SIX CONTEMPORARY DRAMATISTS

Also by Duncan Wu

WORDWORTH'S READING, 1770–1799

ROMANTICISM: An Anthology (*editor*)

WILLIAM WORDSWORTH:
A Selection of his Finest Poems
(*co-editor with Stephen Gill*)

Six Contemporary Dramatists

Bennett, Potter, Gray, Brenton, Hare, Ayckbourn

Duncan Wu

Postdoctoral Fellow of the British Academy
St Catherine's College, Oxford

For John Bayley,
with much gratitude
and all the best.

Duncan Wu

24.1.95

M

St. Martin's Press

First published in Great Britain 1995 by
MACMILLAN PRESS LTD
Houndmills, Basingstoke, Hampshire RG21 2XS
and London
Companies and representatives
throughout the world

A catalogue record for this book is available
from the British Library.

ISBN 0–333–61368–6

10   9   8   7   6   5   4   3   2   1
04   03   02   01   00   99   98   97   96   95

Printed and bound in Great Britain by
Antony Rowe Ltd
Chippenham, Wiltshire

First published in the United States of America 1995 by
Scholarly and Reference Division,
ST. MARTIN'S PRESS, INC.,
175 Fifth Avenue,
New York, N.Y. 10010

ISBN 0–312–12360–4

Library of Congress Cataloging-in-Publication Data
Wu, Duncan.
Six contemporary dramatists—Bennett, Potter, Gray, Brenton, Hare,
Ayckbourn / Duncan Wu.
p. cm.
Includes bibliographical references and index.
ISBN 0–312–12360–4
1. English drama—20th century—History and criticism. I. Title.
PR736.W8 1995
822'.91409—dc20
                                                                94–26330
                                                                CIP

Give me my robe, put on my crown, I have
Immortal longings in me.

Antony and Cleopatra, V, ii, 280–1

Contents

Contents

Acknowledgements

I wish to thank the following for encouraging me, at various times, to think and write about drama: June Cooper, of St Catherine's Drama Studio, Guildford; Lindsay Duguid, of the *Times Literary Supplement*; and Jonathan Wordsworth, of St Catherine's College, Oxford. I am grateful to Nick Hern, for sending me one of the last remaining copies of *Berlin Bertie*, and to Alan Ayckbourn, Cameron Mackintosh Professor of Contemporary Drama at St Catherine's College, Oxford, 1991–2, who discussed his work with me and approved the transcript of the interview published in the Appendix.

While writing this volume I was fortunate in being a Fellow of St Catherine's College, Oxford, and a postdoctoral Fellow of the British Academy. I am grateful to both these institutions for their kind support.

This book is dedicated to Caroline Cochrane.

Oxford   DUNCAN WU

Permissions

1

Introduction: Intangible Commodities

I

This book grew out of my frustration at the absence of any publication designed to explain to my students the concerns that have preoccupied contemporary British dramatists of the 1980s and early 1990s. In a popular field like television and stage drama, such a gap seems all the more surprising. Millions of viewers watched the broadcast plays discussed in following chapters, but little attempt has been made to elucidate them. Similarly, David Hare's *The Secret Rapture* entertained many people when it opened at the National Theatre in London, but its aims are far from transparent, and interpretation seemed to lie beyond the range of most reviewers. Audiences may appreciate some guide to such works, and an indication of their place in each author's development. As with other literary forms, meanings lie beneath the surface of the text, and sometimes we – as theatregoers, actors, directors, or simply as students of the play – may find it helpful to have these outlined. This volume aims to offer such a guide, and in doing so concentrates on works available to the reader in print.

One means by which I have explained these writers' preoccupations is by placing them within a larger literary context. For my purposes, the most important of these is that of English romanticism. Although it would be wrong to cast them all as romantics, the aspirations of the writers discussed here often reflect its influence. Workable definitions of romanticism are thin on the ground, and no wonder: it was never a unified movement in the same way that Imagism became, nor, given the diversity of its component parts (which includes writers as diverse as Byron, Clare, and James Hogg), could it have been. However, I shall argue that romanticism at its most hopeful might be represented by a blank verse passage composed by Wordsworth as part of the conclusion to *The Ruined Cottage* in early 1798:

1

Not useless do I deem
These quiet sympathies with things that hold
An inarticulate language, for the man
Once taught to love such objects as excite
No morbid passions, no disquietude,
No vengeance and no hatred, needs must feel
The joy of that pure principle of love
So deeply that, unsatisfied with aught
Less pure and exquisite, he cannot choose
But seek for objects of a kindred love
In fellow-natures, and a kindred joy.[1]

This is probably Wordsworth's pithiest, and most convinced rehearsal of the argument that love of nature leads to love of mankind, the guiding principle of his unfinished epic poem, *The Recluse*. It depends on a necessitarian principle by which 'inarticulate' forms in the natural world will compel the perceiving mind to seek out 'a kindred love' among others. Ultimately, 'the burthen of existence' – that is, pain and suffering – would be lifted from everyone, and humankind would proceed together in millennial brotherhood. Ludicrous though these ideas may seem to us, Wordsworth was not alone in believing them. Joseph Priestley, the discoverer of oxygen, advanced similar notions, and William Blake went even further.[2] Perhaps it had something to do with the end of the century: Madam Blavatsky preached like doctrines at the end of the next, and more justified intimations of apocalypse are resurfacing now.

What distinguishes Wordsworth is the centrality of these beliefs to virtually everything he composed. And at the heart of his millennial philosophy (inherited largely from Coleridge) he placed an imperative: that the inherently improving effects of nature compel us to behave better towards one other. In *Tintern Abbey* he declared that nature was

The anchor of my purest thoughts, the nurse,
The guide, the guardian of my heart, and soul
Of all my moral being. (lines 110–12)

His closeness to the natural world from boyhood onwards qualified him uniquely for the task of expounding these beliefs to the reading public. So convinced was Coleridge of this that he virtually gave up writing poetry himself, while Wordsworth spent much of his creative life waiting for the millennial heaven on earth and trying to compose the epic that would precipitate it.

It's the moral emphasis that makes Wordsworthian romanticism so pertinent to our reading of contemporary dramatists, and particularly those discussed here. As Brenton observes, 'There is an infinite variety of ways of making theatre, but only one theme which, inevitably, Aeschylus was onto – it's simply "how can we live justly?" '[3] Potter notes an even older source; discussing Arthur Parker, the sheet-music salesman of *Pennies From Heaven*, he notes that 'the songs that he was peddling were in a direct line of descent from the Psalms . . . and what they were saying was that the world is other than it is, the world is better than this'.[4] The sense of fallenness is a universal, and Utopia takes on an added appeal when times are bad. *Pennies From Heaven* is set during the depression of the 1930s – a world not so different from the austere surroundings of Britain in 1978, when it was first broadcast. With the election of Mrs Thatcher and a new era of Conservative rule in 1979, however, life in Britain changed drastically.

For some, Utopia had arrived. Mrs Thatcher set out to reduce state involvement in people's lives, shifting responsibilities that had previously belonged to government onto private business. The effects of this policy were sweeping, particularly in the arts. During the 1960s and 1970s many playwrights, including some of those discussed here, had benefited from state subsidies to theatres and touring companies. During the 1980s, that activity was cut back: like many theatre groups, Foco Novo, who under Roland Rees commissioned *Bloody Poetry* in 1984, dissolved four years later. At the same time, cheap, small-scale productions stopped appearing on television in favour of expensive, prestigious and internationally-saleable films. The BBC and Channel Four now routinely help finance film productions in exchange for screening rights; series of one-off plays of the kind that in the 1960s brought to a wider public the work of such writers as Harold Pinter, David Mercer and Joe Orton are now rare. In the 1970s, Hare's *Wetherby* might, like *Licking Hitler*, have been a 'Play for Today'; in fact, it was produced as a feature film in 1985, funded in part by Channel Four. Thatcherism has had a devastating impact on the means by which drama is produced in Britain, as an increasing emphasis on commercial viability has led, as elsewhere in the arts, to a corresponding reluctance to take risks.

My interest lies less with the changing conditions in which drama is produced, than with the effects of the last decade on the world as seen through the work of established writers. If Bennett, Potter, Gray, Brenton, Hare and Ayckbourn have responded variously to the events of the last 15 years, none has been untouched by them. Some, like Gray and Hare, have sought consolation in notions inherited from the romantics, while others, like Brenton, have become increasingly lacking in hope. At the same time they share a pervasive concern with ethics, both those of the individual and those of society at large.

II

Shakespearean tragedy provides the other important context to which I relate these writers. *Hamlet*, *Othello* and *King Lear* are, of course, enormously influential works, but they have a particular importance here. For instance, between the filming of *Wetherby* and *Paris by Night*, Hare directed a National Theatre production of *King Lear*. Why? Because it shared a number of important features with his own work of the period. In fact, one of the arguments of this book is that these playwrights have either drawn on Shakespeare or redefined tragedy for themselves as their work has evolved. As in Shakespearean tragedy, their plays tend to confront moral judgements with the less determinable facts of human emotion.

One of the characteristics of Shakespearean tragedy is that, although the audience may think that they have a clear under-standing of good and evil, the drama cuts across such distinctions. This is partly because most of his tragic plays centre on the mad or almost mad: Macbeth is disturbed when he kills Duncan, and is certainly unbalanced by the consequences; Othello is crazed because his emotions are undermined; and Hamlet is maddened by Gertrude's marriage to Claudius. Extreme emotional states are outside the ordinary black and white facts of good and evil. As a result we may manage to retain some sympathy for Othello as he smothers Desdemona because we know that he has been deceived, and that he remains, in his own terms, honest even as he does it. It is even possible to remain sympathetic to Macbeth, who is egged on by supernatural forces beyond his control. In short, Shakespeare is concerned to ask what constitutes just behaviour in exceptional circumstances. As Lear asks, 'which is the justice, which is the thief?', concluding that 'Robes and furr'd gowns hide all' (IV, vi, 153–4, 165): if you have authority, your conduct goes unquestioned.

The nature of tragedy is that insights of that kind, however true, cannot alter the course of events. At the end of the play Lear wakes up to a love for Cordelia that appears too vital and immediate ever to perish. 'So we'll live', he tells her,

> and we'll wear out,
> In a wall'd prison, packs and sects of great ones,
> That ebb and flow by th' moon. (V, iii, 11–19)

Engaged in the world of action, politicians are by nature ephemeral, whereas he and Cordelia have a relationship that is immortal. That romantic longing contains its own poetic truth, but Shakespeare confronts it with a reality in which the likes of Edmund can sign death-warrants. Cordelia must be hanged, and Lear survives just long enough to ask, 'Why should a dog, a horse, a rat, have life,/ And thou no breath at all?' (V, iii, 307–8). To which there is no answer, except that such apparent contradictions are essentially tragic. There is a similar moment when Desdemona revives after Othello has attempted to smother her:

EMILIA: O, who hath done this deed?
DESDEMONA: Nobody; I myself. Farewell!
    Commend me to my kind lord. O, farewell! [*Dies.*]

At that instant, the audience realises that Othello has destroyed the one person who might have saved him – someone who loved him so much that, on the point of death, she was prepared to conceal his crime. That painful understanding is heightened by his exclamation a few lines later: 'She's like a liar gone to burning hell:/ 'Twas I that kill'd her' (V, ii, 123–30). Tragedy is the removal of what is ultimately precious – a perception that is by nature fleeting; it is less a question of form or style, than of moments of intense emotional precipitation. If a drama climaxes in this way, it may be regarded as an accomplished tragedy.

This reading of Shakespeare is unashamedly romantic in valuing emotion over morality – and it is, for that reason, relevant to a reading of the writers discussed here. Though on the run, Frank and Cecily, the star-crossed lovers of Brenton's novel, *Diving for Pearls*, are redeemed by their love: 'They had much fun', one character remarks, 'Romantisch. They were romantic.' Against the injustice envisioned by the novel, from the British occupation of Northern Ireland to the betrayals practised by Brenton's characters, the truth of Frank and Cecily's love vindicates them, just as intense feeling ratifies Lear and Cordelia in the face of brutality.

In Shakespeare, there is also a distinction between the deaths of the victim and the protagonist. We may grieve at the fates of Desdemona and Cordelia, but the deaths of Othello and Lear are far less charged. Othello kills himself quite satisfactorily in an act of justice, while Lear dies deluded and happy, believing that Cordelia lives. Cleopatra dies acting out the mother/child relationship with the asp that is to kill her: 'Dost thou not see my baby at my breast,/ That sucks the nurse asleep?' (V, ii, 308–9). The comparison is poignant but reassuring. As she herself points out, it is a more desirable fate than to be exhibited as a spoil of victory. The protagonist's death is irrelevant to the nature of tragedy. It is no more than a release, a loss of consciousness, without emotional value:

> Vex not his ghost. O, let him pass, he hates him
> That would upon the rack of this tough world
> Stretch him out longer. (V, iii, 314–16)

Self-realisation plays no part in Shakespearean tragedy. Lear's only understanding at the end of his life lies in the need for love – a love which is removed from him, and thus forms the substance of his tragedy.

Brenton and Hare have both learned from Shakespeare's handling of death. Frank and Cecily in *Diving for Pearls* are dispatched in a sentence: 'Peter Carter's machine pistol fired so quickly, that their deaths were virtually simultaneous.'[5] The event has been anticipated for a long time, and is far less interesting than the passion which it brings to an end. The more complex implications for Hare's *The Secret Rapture* are discussed, pp. 108–9, below.

Influence is not always straightforward. But the writers discussed here have either adopted Shakespearean concepts of tragedy, or redefined them for their own purposes. Tragedy in Ayckbourn's or Bennett's work tends to be determined less by intensity of emotion than by situation, and thus depends more on the characters' moral judgements than on the interventions of an unjust world. All the same, that distinction can be appreciated only in the context of the Shakespearean model.

III

Not all of the writers discussed here are romantics, and not all of them are tragedians, but it is in relation to those literary precedents – familiar to everyone – that I wish to locate them. Romanticism and tragedy are appropriate to a discussion of literature during the 1980s partly because they stand at opposite emotional extremes – and extremity was characteristic of the age. In *Serious Money* (1987), Caryl Churchill captured both the exuberance and cynicism of the 1980s in a drama that combined elements of romance with those of tragedy. More pointedly still, a writer as sensitive to the spirit of the age as Howard Brenton has turned, during the course of the 1980s, from idealism to despair. In the third section of this Introduction I wish to look briefly at the way in which each of the writers discussed here has developed in recent years.

The profound scepticism that underlies Bennett's work is suggested by the fact that George Oliver, the alienated MP of *Getting On* (1971), works for the Labour Party. Bennett remarks that he is 'so self-absorbed that he remains blind to the fact that his wife is having an affair with the handyman, his mother-in-law is dying, his son is getting ready to leave home, his best friend thinks him a fool and that to everyone who comes into contact with him he is a self-esteeming joke'.[6] Bennett's protagonists typically lack the awareness that would enable them to comprehend their foibles, and rectify the wrongs they inadvertently commit against others. Tunnel vision is their besetting sin, and it usually implies a more profound failure. George's best friend, Brian, is the only one to suggest what this might be:

> Come close and you'll see a scar. We've all had an operation. We've been seen to, doctored, like cats. Some essential part of our humanity has been removed. It's not honesty or straightforward-ness, or the usual things politicians are supposed to lack. It's a sense of the ridiculous, the bloody pointlessness of it all, that's what they've lost. They think they're important. As if it mattered.[7]

The exercise of power has rendered George morally bankrupt; according to him, 'ninety per cent of the people in this world are thick', and it is his job to lead them – by the nose, if need be.[8] His belief that his life is meaningful because he controls others prevents him from accepting Brian's argument that the world is arbitrary,

random and, as he puts it, pointless. That sense of the ridiculous is
not constricting; on the contrary, it is regarded throughout Bennett's
work as a means of liberation. Deaf to Brian's admonitions, George
remains a prisoner of his own fiction of self-importance, proving,
along with his estrangement from family and friends, and his
totalitarian assumptions, his son's assessment: 'You're a killer, Dad,
you really are.'[9]

Written just after the fall of the Wilson government, *Getting On*
implied a bitter disillusionment with the Labour Party and those
within it. By 1987, when the prospect of Labour victory was remote,
and the Thatcherite boom was in full swing, Bennett's emphasis had
shifted. In place of the cynicism of *Getting On*, he sought to reassess
idealism in plays about Guy Burgess and Anthony Blunt, *An
Englishman Abroad* and *A Question of Attribution*. He could hardly
have chosen two men about whose conduct the British public were
more decided. For years, Philby, Burgess, Maclean and Blunt had
been held up as traitors by the government and the national press,
and the label had stuck. Bennett's case is that such judgements
educate the populace in the cause of a hypocritical and repressive
ideology; in fact he goes out of his way to note that 'Blunt and
Burgess and co. had the advantage of us in that they still had
illusions.'[10] At a time when idealism was long out of fashion,
Bennett proclaimed its worth. The commercial success of *Single Spies*
(shared by other plays critical of the age, including Brenton and
Hare's *Pravda*[11] and Caryl Churchill's *Serious Money*) shouldn't be
allowed to obscure its radicalism. In fact, Bennett's concern with
hypocrisy, and the corruption of principled people when they gain
power, is also the subject of Brenton's *Thirteenth Night* and *Bloody
Poetry*.

Bennett has noted the recurrence of hospitals in his plays,[12] and
that fact alerts us to his relevance to a discussion of latter-day
romantics; as Potter observes, betrayal of one's ideals is built into
the human organism: 'as your own body betrays you, as you age, so
the purity (for instance) of a political belief can be fortunately
temporised by . . . the rough and tumble of life. The falling away of
belief and the falling away of commitment, while partly inevitable,
still tears the flesh away from the bone.'[13] If Potter does not offer a
specifically ideological drama, he is searching for the correct
response to a society which, as he says, is 'about selling all of you
to all of you. . . . [in which] the only object is to keep in the game, to
keep selling something.'[14] His recent protagonists are dispossessed,

exiled from Thatcher's paradise, disgusted by the stink of its corruption, and demoralised by its assault on the individual. Having dropped out of the game, they retreat into themselves. Most notably, Philip Marlow in *The Singing Detective* undertakes that most romantic journey into the underworld of his past, where he forges a unity out of the half-memories, associations, repressed images and symbols, and emerges with a new sense of identity: the wounds caused by the betrayal of our early visions *can* be healed. There is nothing conservative about such introspection; Potter's reaffirmation of the individual consciousness is acutely subversive of the free market's totalising vision. *Lipstick on Your Collar* (1993), his most recent television serial, affirms that deeply-felt radicalism. Set during the Suez crisis, it reveals a Britain divided by class, and imprisoned by assumptions left over from its imperial past. The only way forward is to embrace Americanisation – including that of its innocent Welsh protagonist, who is paired off with the daughter of a Texas oil baron.

Although Gray's concern with politics is less overt than Potter's, *Melon* (1987), later rewritten as *The Holy Terror* (1989), satirises the orgiastic abandon that typified the euphoria of the eighties boom. *Melon* is identical in kind to such characters as Butley, Simon Hench, and Peter in *Plaintiffs and Defendants* (1975) – all of them emotionally alienated. He is distinguished by his extremity, which in turn roots the play in the 1980s. Locked into a frenetic round of business lunches, shady deals and compulsive philandering, he rides high on his own self-esteem until the inevitable breakdown – a career that exemplifies the cycle of brilliance and burnout so characteristic of the age. As he discovers, success *is* illness. But his real problem is a detachment from ethical standards:

> But you see, ladies, please believe me, you must believe me, please, when I say . . . (*Stares towards them*) that I still don't know what the truth is. No, I don't. (*Shakes his head*) That's still my problem. That I've had the experience, you see. But as the poet, some poet, famous poet, said, had the experience but missed the meaning.[15]

To make moral points with such certainty you have to believe, as Gray does, in absolutes; and perhaps more so than any other writer discussed here, he employs romantically-derived images and ideas as his points of reference. At the same time, the coded discourse of literary allusion reflects the unworldliness of those who speak it. Only because Stuart in *The Common Pursuit* is 'Genuinely in love, genuinely loving',[16] is he vulnerable to the abuse of those he trusts. By the same token St John Quartermaine, the most enlightened of Gray's mystics, goes unrecognised as such and is not in any case competent to communicate his insights to those around him. The central image of *Quartermaine's Terms* (1983) may allude to Yeats' *Wild Swans at Coole*, but it is ignored by everyone.

If Gray is too pragmatic to allow romanticism to change the world as seen in his plays, he is too sensitive not to perceive that failure as a kind of tragedy. As with Lear, who hails the new-found love between himself and Cordelia as immortal even as Edmund condemns Cordelia to the gallows, so such characters as Stuart and Quartermaine, virtuous though they may be, cannot protect themselves from the treachery of those closest to them. Indeed, the most powerful and compelling of Gray's characters are his villains. It is no surprise that he was drawn to Molière's *Tartuffe*, which he adapted in 1982. Like Nick in *The Common Pursuit*, Tartuffe knows how to get on in the midst of corruption and, like Bonny in *The Rear Column*, he manipulates others for his own ends. Gray's theme is the denial rather than the acknowledgement of ethical standards; the closest he comes to stating it explicitly is in *Tartuffe*, when Cléante tells his brother-in-law, Orgon: 'Look, there's no clarity like blindness, don't you see? Blindness to life and all you love – that's what Tartuffe's done to you, made you blind, d'you see?'[17] As Cléante observes, the apparent lucidity of delusion is what makes it so hard to acknowledge.

If lack of self-awareness is the enabling device of the morality play, its recovery (or not) is a crucial determinant of tone. In this light, Gray's recent work has been less pessimistic than that of the 1970s, when he was content to leave such characters as Butley and Hench suspended in an atrophy of the spirit. Despite their disgruntlement at human nature, *The Common Pursuit*, *Tartuffe*, *Melon* and *Hidden Laughter* leave room for hope, because Gray has foregrounded his belief in the absolutes denied by the prevailing agnosticism of the age. *Hidden Laughter* may teeter on the brink of tragedy, but its protagonist's concluding speech combines wishful-ness with dismay:

Everything will be as it always has been and all my memories of all our summers will join up into one summer, with all the dark spots gone. And all the summers still to come already joining up in memory and anticipation – oh, Harry, darling Harry – (*Stops, unable to go on because she is crying; it is not clear whether from happiness or grief, no longer reading.*) Why have we been away from each other for so long! Why have we?[18]

As in the final moments of Hare's *The Secret Rapture*, the elegiac note is coloured by a wistful yearning for a better world. Gray shares with Hare and Brenton a refusal to capitulate to despair. Possibilities may have closed down in the past, but they may still be projected into the future.

Although Brenton's work has become darker in recent years, his aims have not changed since he remarked in 1980 that 'I write for the conventional reasons . . . for peace, a weapon of peace, to change the world, to encourage the good and discourage the bad.'[19] That determined idealism coexists with a bleakly oppressive sense of the outside world – a component even of his earliest work. 'Liberation City?' Veronica asks her fellow-revolutionaries in *Magnificence* (1973), the tenth day of their squat taking a turn for the worse. 'Direct action? For us it's come down to sitting on a stinking lavatory for ten days . . . Why didn't we get the local people on our side? Oh we bawled a few slogans at passers-by. Got the odd turd back from the street, and philosophised there upon. But "Mobilize the people?" We can't mobilize a tin opener . . .'[20] For a pragmatist like Brenton, the failure of a just revolution in Britain must be bitterly disappointing, and much of his work is devoted to explaining it. One of his most important plays in this respect is *The Romans in Britain* (1980), which traces the moral weakness of British people back to the Roman invasion. The Saxons of AD 515 reveal that the Romans have sent a Bishop from Rome to teach them 'that we're born in sin. Even in the cradle, bad. Filthy.'[21] Marban, the Celtic priest of 54 BC is even more certain that, as he tells his people,

you'll never dig out the fear they've struck in you. With their strange, foreign weapons.

Generation after generation, cataracts of terror in the eyes of your children. And in the eyes of husband for wife and wife for husband, hatred of the suffering that is bound to come again.[22]

The divisive principle that has alienated people from their best instincts reverberates throughout Brenton's plays. Thomas Chichester, the English army officer doing undercover work in present-day Northern Ireland, recognises that the Celtic way of life is attuned to 'A sense – of the order – of things',[23] a natural, social and political order displaced by the oppositional ways of the Romans, and which the present-day Britons have inherited. Brenton's critique of the British can be traced back to *Christie in Love* (1970) and finds its most memorable expression in a speech by Shelley in *Bloody Poetry* (1984): 'Well, England! You neighbours, police committees, censors, you "tut-tutters", you indignant dignitaries, parliamentaries, thin-lipped pedlars of smug moralities, I give you what you want, a shit-smeared bum'.[24] So inextricably trapped is Shelley in the role which the establishment have assigned him that he sees no option but to play it. This uneasy defeatism has always been a crucial facet of Brenton's vision; it is, for instance, the believers in his work who die – Christie, Chichester (who is 'a romantic and a bloody menace'),[25] Cecily and Frank in *Diving for Pearls*.

The inbuilt resistance to revolution does not account fully for the grimness of Brenton's more recent work. Such works as *H.I.D. (Hess is Dead)* (1989), *Moscow Gold* (1990) and *Berlin Bertie* (1992) attempt to find an appropriate response to the collapse of the totalitarian *ancien régime* in Eastern Europe. Thanks to a firmly-grounded pragmatism that will not allow his own just nature to obscure the clarity with which he perceives the world, Brenton has been prompt to acknowledge the rise of nationalism in Germany and the problems entailed by unification. Hare has described the imagination as 'the most dangerous place to go for any story',[26] one reason being that it often forces us to apprehend what we would prefer to overlook. Any writer who wishes to be truly responsive to their vision must be fearless in its pursuit. As this suggests, Hare and Brenton have assumed a romantic view of imaginative process; introducing his latest work, Brenton notes that 'Coleridge described the imagination as a well, into which stories, experiences, half-heard phrases are thrown; they stick to each other, like the hooks and eyes of burrs, and change; then when you draw them up to the light, memories have formed themselves into something else . . . Mmm. Yes, it is like that.'[27]

Brenton has spoken enthusiastically of what he describes as 'a meeting of antibodies',[28] when his ideas are opposed by collaborators. His most successful partnership has been with David Hare, with whom he has written *Brassneck* (1973) and *Pravda* (1985). It is curious, given the coincidence of their views on theatre, that their respective developments during the 1980s have been in opposing directions. Against Brenton's unconsoled realism, the faith that informs such early Hare works as *Knuckle* (1974) has been sustained. Hare's archetypal protagonist is a virtuous woman attached to some person or cause which she has idealised: Sarah (*Knuckle*); Anna (*Licking Hitler*); Susan (*Plenty*); Jean (*Wetherby*); Isobel (*The Secret Rapture*); Irina (*Murmuring Judges*). His only outright villainness – Clara Paige MP in *Paris by Night* (1988) – is characterised by a contempt for humane values such that she does not hesitate to kill a man she suspects (wrongly, as it turns out) of blackmailing her. On her election she recalls the latent fascism of another politician, George Oliver, when she tells her supporters that 'People are crying out to be led.'[29] It is left to her lover, Wallace, to tell her of the void within: 'You're corrupt. You have no character. That's your real curse. Words come out, but there's nothing in you.'[30] *Paris by Night* is part of an investigation into the effects of Thatcherism on life in Britain that began with *The Secret Rapture* (1988). Hare's recent trilogy has become more specific in this quest, and has assumed the topicality of a news report: *Racing Demon* examines the rise of evangelism; *Murmuring Judges* deals with legal reform; *The Absence of War* asks why the Labour Party lost the 1992 general election. In fact, each of these plays grew out of contemporary research, which Hare has published as *Asking Around: Background to the David Hare Trilogy* (1993).

'Judgement is at the heart of the theatre', Hare believes,[31] and both he and Brenton regard drama as a means of helping us analyse the affairs of our own time. If the other writers discussed in this volume are no less subversive, Hare is distinguished by the demands he makes on his audiences, for whatever one's own political views you can't simply dismiss the issues he raises. But the value of his work lies not just in its provocativeness; among these writers, he seems secure in his belief in a transcendent idealism that Wordsworth would have recognised immediately – in fact, the culminating speech of *Racing Demon* (1990) derives its imagery from the Climbing of Snowdon in *Prelude* Book XIII.[32] Unlike Brenton, he defiantly refuses to despair, preserving a kernel of optimism in even his darkest work.

Like Brenton and Hare, Ayckbourn has been profoundly affected by the materialism of the 1980s. He is not usually considered a political writer, but his plays of the last ten years have sought to address the moral decay that has accompanied Thatcherism. As he remarks: 'Although it's true that I write about individuals rather than issues, you could say, for "a small family business" read "a whole nation state". It isn't that it's just a family, it goes further and wider than that.'[33] Unlike the other writers here, Ayckbourn is not a University graduate, which may help explain why he draws less on the literary heritage. In spite of this – or perhaps because of it – he is the only one to offer a genuinely post-romantic response to Thatcherism. Having abandoned the model of humanity favoured by the other writers here – that of a flawed spirit capable of ideal construction – Ayckbourn offers something different: purely physical beings who may or may not choose to aspire to higher things. The driving force of idealism that lies at the heart of the romantic vision has been exchanged for a more material conception of human life. In that respect Ayckbourn finds Mrs Thatcher a fitting representative of the people: 'She embodies what the majority of this country believe, and aim for, and strive for. She's there because they put her there, or somebody put her there . . . . You get what you deserve. She was our representative on earth, really – what we all jointly created.'[34] Not that Ayckbourn himself finds this agreeable: 'You can't reduce everything in the end to a profit sheet', he has said. This conviction has led him to focus on the intangible commodities overlooked by the free market, but with none of the consolation other writers have found. Had Ayckbourn written *The Secret Rapture* Marion would not have come to her senses in the final scene because it partakes of an idealism which he does not recognise. And yet he belongs here because his most recent work still manages to accommodate hope, earthbound and recessed though it may be.

As we approach our own *fin de siècle* we become more aware of the need for a unifying mythology similar to that concocted by the early romantics, one that might resolve the lassitude and dislocation of contemporary society. It is a bitter irony that, as that need grows, the capacity for belief of any kind becomes increasingly attenuated. Wordsworth and Coleridge were fortunate in living at a time when, in spite of the failure of the French Revolution, it was possible to think that paradise might be reclaimed by an act of faith. That no one in their right mind would subscribe to such notions today only underlines the spiritual poverty of the age; we are reduced to picking through the rubble and salvaging what we can. The fact that the dramatists whose work is analysed here continue to write at all represents a colossal act of faith. Unfashionable though it may be, they have chosen to write morality plays, and that you can do only if you believe that drama can change people's lives for the better. As such, they are the inheritors of a deeply-ingrained romanticism which, despite its fragility, may be all that separates us from the apocalypse foreseen by Yeats:

> The blood-dimmed tide is loosed, and everywhere
> The ceremony of innocence is drowned;
> The best lack all conviction, while the worst
> Are full of passionate intensity.[35]

2

Alan Bennett:
Anarchists of the Spirit

In a speech deleted from the final version of Alan Bennett's *The Madness of George III* (1991), the King makes an important observation which, Bennett says, is 'the nearest I can get to extracting a message from the play':

> The real lesson, if I may say so, is that what makes an illness perilous is celebrity. Or, as in my case, royalty. In the ordinary course of things doctors want their patients to recover; their reputations depend on it. But if the patient is rich or royal, powerful or famous, other considerations enter in. There are many parties interested apart from the interested party. So more doctors are called in and none but the best will do. But the best aren't always very good and they argue, they disagree. They have to because they are after all the best and the world is watching. And who is in the middle? The patient. It happened to me. It happened to Napoleon. It happened to Anthony Eden. It happened to the Shah. The doctors even killed off George V to make the first edition of *The Times*. I tell you, dear people, if you're poorly it's safer to be poor and ordinary.[1]

Only in the wake of severe illness does the King realise that the political power that gives him such freedom is in reality a prison. As King, he is confined within a role; indeed, the play gives less time to his illness which, as Bennett admits, 'is of no dramatic consequence',[2] than to the responses of those around him. The Prince of Wales and his allies attempt to take political advantage while the royal doctors literally torture his father with their supposed cures. Be that as it may, George III is one of the lucky ones. Not only does he gain some measure of self-awareness but he is granted an interval of idealistic sanity in which to heal the rift between himself and his son: 'For the future, we must try to be more of a family. There are model farms now, model villages, even model factories. Well, we must be a model family for the nation to look on.'[3]

Our own monarch, Queen Elizabeth II, suffers a similar confinement in *A Question of Attribution* (1988). At one point the Keeper of the Queen's Paintings, Anthony Blunt, admits that he is an expert on Poussin.

> HMQ: Poussin. French for chicken. One has just had it for lunch. I suppose it's fresh in the mind. It was one of what I call my All Walks of Life luncheons. Today we had the head of the CBI, an Olympic swimmer, a primary school headmistress, a General in the Salvation Army, and Glenda Jackson. It was a bit sticky.
>
> BLUNT: I've been to one, Ma'am. That was a bit sticky, too.
>
> HMQ: The trouble is, whenever I meet anybody they're always on their best behaviour. And when one is on one's best behaviour one isn't always at one's best. I don't understand it. They all have different jobs, there ought to be heaps to talk about, yet I'm always having to crank it up.[4]

Trapped in her role as inextricably as Blunt is in his, HMQ is condemned always to encounter people on their best behaviour; similarly, Blunt is doomed for the remainder of his life to meet those hungry for information about his past. Set before his unmasking in 1978 when, as Bennett writes, 'I felt more sympathy with the hunted than the hunters',[5] the play is full of reminders that Blunt's present way of life cannot continue for much longer.

He has periodic meetings with Chubb, a member of the Intelligence Service, to whom he relates his history. 'You must understand that your situation does not improve with time,' Chubb remarks in the final scene, 'More and more questions are being asked. The wolves, if you like, are getting closer. We may have to throw you off our sledge now. The consequences will be embarrassing, and not only for you. For us too. It will be painful. You will be the object of scrutiny, explanations sought after, your history gone into. You will be named. Attributed.'[6] Chubb's choice of words is all important. Attributions and conjectures will be made about Blunt's past in the same way that scholars and critics interpret what lies beneath the encrusted dirt and varnish of old canvases. As a former academic himself, having embarked on a doctoral dissertation on the household of Richard II in Oxford during the 1950s, Bennett is well acquainted with the built-in myopia of the scholarly pursuit.[7]

In Blunt's case, the gap between supposition and fact is immense. As he tells Chubb, 'Art history is seldom thought of as a hazardous profession. But a life spent teasing out riddles of this kind carries its own risks . . . a barrenness of outlook, a pedantry that verges on the obsessive, and a farewell to commonsense; the rule of the hobby horse. Because, though the solution might add to our appreciation of this painting, paintings, we must never forget, are not there primarily to be solved. A great painting will still elude us, as art will always elude exposition.'[8] In this sense, great paintings are not unlike life, since we should not assume that a retrospective judgement can have any but a prejudiced bearing on lived experience. We are as much prisoners of our own values as Blunt is of his past.

He cautions Chubb, who is using their acquaintance as a means of learning about art, against looking harshly on minor artists:

BLUNT: These painters – Giotto, Piero – they aren't so many failed Raphaels, Leonardos without the know-how. Try to look at them as contemporaries did, judge them on their own terms, not as prefiguring some (to them) unknown future. They didn't know Raphael was going to do it better.

CHUBB: To be quite honest I haven't got to Raphael. But where have I heard that argument before?[9]

Blunt proposes not just a technique for the study of art; nothing could be more politically subversive than our complicity with another age. Such an approach represents the triumph not so much of the critical faculty but of the imagination, and in this Bennett is nothing if not romantic. To perceive the artistic achievement of the most minor artist is to partake of something more lasting and valuable than mere fact.

An Englishman Abroad, the companion play to *A Question of Attribution*, deals with the same theme. Guy Burgess, uncomfortably settled in his Moscow flat, cuts a pathetic figure when the actress Coral Browne visits him while touring the Soviet Union with a production of *Hamlet*. While the play makes no bones about the spy's hardship in exile it is concerned more with the reasons for his flight from Britain. After their meeting Browne returns to London where, as a favour, she attempts vainly to buy Burgess a pair of pyjamas:

ASSISTANT: I'm afraid, madam, that the gentleman in question no longer has an account with us. His account was closed.
CORAL: I know. He wishes to open it again.
ASSISTANT: I'm afraid that's not possible.
CORAL: Why?
ASSISTANT: Well . . . we supply pyjamas to the Royal Family.
CORAL: So?
ASSISTANT: The gentleman is a traitor, madam.
CORAL: So? Must traitors sleep in the buff?
ASSISTANT: I'm sorry. We have to draw the line somewhere.
CORAL: So why here? Say someone commits adultery in your precious nightwear. I imagine it has occurred. What happens when he comes in to order his next pair of jim-jams? Is it sorry, no can do?
ASSISTANT: I'm very sorry.
CORAL: (*Her Australian accent gets now more pronounced as she gets crosser*) You keep saying you're sorry, dear. You were quite happy to satisfy this client when he was one of the most notorious buggers in London and a drunkard into the bargain. Only then he was in the Foreign Office. 'Red piping on the sleeve, Mr Burgess – but of course.' 'A discreet monogram on the pocket, Mr Burgess? Certainly. And perhaps if you'd be gracious enough to lower your trousers, Mr Burgess, we could be privileged enough to thrust our tongue between the cheeks of your arse.' But not any more. Oh no. Because the gentleman in question has shown himself to have some principles, principles which aren't yours and, as a matter of interest, aren't mine. But that's it, as far as you're concerned. No more jamas for him. I tell you, it's pricks like you that make me understand why he went. Thank Christ I'm not English.[10]

The Assistant's argument, with its condonement of buggery and condemnation of idealism, is an insult to the morality it pretends to uphold. But that does not quite explain why Browne gets so upset with him. In fact his real sin is the failure of his imagination. Bound by values he has been taught not to question, he is denied even the lucid intervals granted George III. 'I don't know what treachery means', Bennett declared in a BBC interview in 1983. 'People commit treason and get rewarded for it . . . . Treason is just a word.'[11] In his introduction to *Single Spies* he goes further, suggesting that idealism of any kind makes betrayal of one's country hard to avoid: 'Of course Blunt and Burgess and co. had the advantage of us in that they still had illusions. They had somewhere to turn. The trouble with treachery nowadays is that if one does want to betray one's country there is no one satisfactory to betray it to. If there were, more people would be doing it.'[12]

The desire to escape, whether from the dullness of one's country, madness, or the past, provides the essentially romantic impulse behind all of Bennett's work. Confronted with the challenge of transforming John Lahr's biography of Joe Orton, *Prick Up Your Ears*, into a film script, it is not surprising that he framed it as the story of Orton's failure to escape his unhappy 'marriage' with his lover, Kenneth Halliwell. As he observes, 'To be stuck in the same room as Kenneth Halliwell for fifteen years can have been no joke.'[13]

Other spiritual anarchists include Susan, the vicar's wife in *Bed Among the Lentils* (one of Bennett's *Talking Heads* monologues). Trapped in a loveless marriage to a pious husband, she ends up having an affair with an Asian grocer, Mr Ramesh, 'who once, on the feast of St Simon and St Jude (Choral Evensong at six, daily services at the customary hour), put make-up on his eyes and bells on his ankles, and naked except for his little belt danced in the back room of his shop with a tambourine'.[14] Invoked after Susan's return to her husband and his devoted congregation, this exotic image is a reminder both of her brief triumph, and of a better life she has yet to begin.

Like Susan, Denis Midgley, the protagonist of the 1982 television play *Intensive Care*, is unhappily married. While at the bedside of his dying father in hospital, he encounters Alice Duckworth, a rich widow with whom his father had an affair during his last years. 'You go your own way', she advises him.[15] His response to the discovery of an unsuspected bohemian streak in his father is to seduce Valery, one of the nurses. As he gets into bed with her, he remarks: 'It's what people call living, is this. We're living. I ought to have done more of this.' And after they have made love he turns to her and says: 'That was a risk. Still, we are now going to be taking risks. The new, risky life of D. Midgley.'[16] After his father's death he returns to his everyday routine, but with an added danger: he has taken up smoking.

Trevor Hopkins, the protagonist of the 1978 play *Me, I'm afraid of Virginia Woolf*, finds liberation of a different kind. Trevor teaches an evening course on the Bloomsbury Group at the Mechanics' Institute in Halifax. In one scene he lectures his class on Woolf:

> In general her books are very decorous. They're concerned with feelings, impressions rather than actions. In the novels of Virginia Woolf we do not expect to come across a scantily clad blonde standing over a body with a smoking gun in her hand. Any more than in the novels of E.M. Forster do we follow a trail of discarded undies towards the bedroom. Undies do not lead to bedrooms or marriage to mayhem. But supposing they did would this be any more Life than a middle-aged lady sitting reading in a garden?

Trevor doesn't answer this question out loud but in a voice-over says 'Yes. Yes. It would.'[17] The literary point may be well-founded – that Woolf and Forster fail to penetrate to the heart of life because they themselves were constrained, undeclared. But Trevor's remarks are more important for what they reveal of himself. The voice-over gives the game away: it is Trevor who is undeclared. As in *Mrs Dalloway*, the play's turning point comes in its final moment, when Trevor looks at Dave, one of his students, and, in the words of the stage directions, we realise 'that this has been a love story'. Unlike Woolf and Forster, Trevor experiences the awful daring of a moment's surrender, at which point, as Bennett writes, 'the music from *South Pacific* swells'.

> I'm not ashamed to reveal
> The world-famous feeling I feel
>
> I'm as corny as Kansas in August,
> I'm as normal as blueberry pie,
> No more a smart little girl with no heart,
> I have found me a wonderful guy!
>
> I am in a conventional dither
> With a conventional star in my eye.
> And you will note there's a lump in my throat
> When I speak of that wonderful guy!

I'm as trite and as gay as a daisy in May,
A cliché coming true!
I'm bromidic and bright as a moon-happy night,
Pouring light on the dew!

I'm as corny as Kansas in August,
High as a flag on the Fourth of July!
If you'll excuse an expression I use,
I'm in love, I'm in love, I'm in love, I'm in love,
I'm in love with a wonderful guy![18]

Lorenz Hart's camped up lyrics drop incongruously into Trevor's bleak, northern milieu. It is a daring effect which succeeds in turning an otherwise sad, dull little play on its head, evoking all the intensity and vividness of love as it appears in the movies. The fact that its context is further distinguished from that of *South Pacific* in alerting us to one man's recognition of his attraction for another only heightens the sensation of unexpectedness, giving rise to an amused optimism. It is no accident that an act of love is also the means by which Denis Midgley and Susan find emancipation. And in doing so, they defy the opprobrium they know their sinfulness would excite.[19]

That moral and religious guilt should be the major deterrent to self-realisation is particularly significant in the context of the personal mythology by which Bennett prefaces his work. As he reveals in his introduction to *Talking Heads*, his mother was the agent by which he first absorbed these inhibitions, which found expression in her harsh moral judgements. In particular, he examines her use of the word 'common': 'A common woman was likely to swear or drink (or drink "shorts"), to get all dolled up and go out leaving the house upside down and make no bones about having affairs. Enjoy herself, possibly, and that was the trouble; a common woman sidestepped her share of the proper suffering of her sex.'[20] By the terms of this unforgiving ethos, suffering must be shared round equally, and those who evade it punished. This explains the compulsive value judgements of Bennett's characters; whether it is Trevor Hopkins' mother claiming to have had a lesbian affair with Aunty Phyllis, or a shop assistant ascribing treachery to Guy Burgess, the aim is to arouse one's sense of moral superiority. In this light one of the wisest of Bennett's characters is Trevor's doctor, who reproves a student colleague, Willard, for admitting that he might be happy:

Willard. You are young. But in this matter of happiness it has been my experience that we none of us wish to be told of the happiness of others. It does not help, Willard. Confess to misery, say one's life is futile, hail the onset of bankruptcy, yes, Willard, because nothing encourages one's fellows more. They go away smiling. But say, 'I am happy. I am having a good time.' No, Willard. The spirit plummets.[21]

Trevor's doctor articulates a conceit that provides some of the best lines in Bennett's plays: everyday life for most people is so miserable that they're happy only when reminded of others' suffering. Take, for instance, Trevor's mother, who remarks in one of the most memorable lines in modern drama: 'I see the President of Romania's mother's died. There's always trouble for somebody.'[22] Elsewhere Bennett describes how northern women believe that 'Hopes are doomed to be dashed, expectations not to be realized, because that's the way God, who certainly speaks with a southern accent, has arranged things.'[23] Not very surprisingly, this unconsoled view of life is frequently embodied by mothers in Bennett's plays; in one of the funniest scenes in *Me, I'm afraid of Virginia Woolf* Trevor is visited at the evening school canteen by his, who is intent on meeting his girlfriend, Wendy.

> MRS HOPKINS: She shouldn't wear trousers.
> HOPKINS: Who?
> MRS HOPKINS: Your girl.
> HOPKINS: She's not 'my girl'. I don't have a girl. She's just somebody I . . .
> MRS HOPKINS: Somebody you what?
> HOPKINS: Somebody I know.
> MRS HOPKINS: Yes. I know too. Somebody you carry on with.
> HOPKINS: Mam, I'm 35.
> MRS HOPKINS: Don't tell me. By the time I was 35 I was married and two children.[24]

Mrs Hopkins is put out less by her son's failure to get married than by his 'carrying on'; it is, in her terms, irresponsible and selfish. This potent cocktail of jealousy and disapprobation culminates when she kisses him goodbye in front of Wendy and then laboriously wipes the lipstick off his face. Another of Bennett's reminiscences analyses his own mother's possessiveness and how, when he was a teenager, while taking communion in church, she led him to fear contracting VD from the chalice:

> With the church chock-a-block with publicans and sinners one never knew who was going to be one's drinking companion. It was all my mother's fault. She brought us up never to share a lemonade bottle with other boys, and wiping it with your hand, she said, was no protection, so I knew the dainty dab with the napkin the priest gave the chalice made no difference at all. There was God of course, in whose omnipotence I was supposed to believe: He might run to some mystical antisepsis. But then He might not. That I should catch syphilis from the chalice might be all part of His plan. The other place I was frightened of contracting it was the seat of a public lavatory, and that the rim of the toilet should be thus linked with the rim of the chalice was also part of the wonderful mystery of God.[25]

God has been dragged down to earth, as throughout Bennett's work human aspirations usually are, by a frigid morality allied to sexual fear. His mother's part in this reminds us that his protagonists are characteristically unable to break out of their mother's clutches. Perhaps the most extreme example of this is Les, the 17-year-old in the 1982 television play, *Marks*. When his mother catches him in bed with a girl she humiliates and chides him: 'You haven't even got started. You haven't even found your feet and now you're off on that game. You're never going to get anywhere now.'[26] Her browbeating has an effect, for the final scene of the play reveals that he has become a homosexual.

Les is one of those characters beaten down by the philosophy of denial. Others include Irene Ruddock, the obsessive letter-writer in *A Lady of Letters* whose harsh judgements lead her to prison. One of the most unsettling moments in Bennett's work comes at the end of the play when, incarcerated in her cell, she tells us:

> Sometimes Bridget will wake up in the middle of the night shouting, dreaming about the kiddy she killed, and I go over and sit by the bed and hold her hand till she's gone off again. There's my little clock ticking and I can hear the wind in the poplar trees by the playing field and maybe it's raining and I'm sitting there. And I'm so *happy*.[27]

So divorced from humanity has Irene become that only in jail can she begin to make contact with others. The admonition implied by the ticking clock and the slightly sinister image of poplar trees in the rain serve to heighten the bleakness of it all, and her derangement is confirmed by the happiness they give her. *A Lady of Letters* constitutes a kind of rake's progress; like that of the eighteenth-century rake, Irene's failure is moral, stemming from a profound insensitivity. She is guilty, for instance, of writing poison pen letters to the couple across the road, accusing them of not taking proper care of their child. One day she receives a visit from a policewoman:

> She said didn't I appreciate this was a caring young couple? I said if they were a caring young couple why did you never see the kiddy? If they were a caring young couple why did they go gadding off every night, leaving the kiddy alone in the house? She said because the kiddy wasn't alone in the house. The kiddy wasn't in the house. The kiddy was in a hospital in Bradford, that's where they were going every night. And that's where the kiddy died, last Friday. I said, 'What of? Neglect?' She said, 'No. Leukaemia.'[28]

Few writers are so adept at exploiting the emotional impact of understatement. Only at the very end of this speech do we realise that we are listening to someone conditioned totally by prejudice and assumption. Moreover, her unruffled delivery indicates that she remains oblivious of her appalling behaviour; in case we are in doubt she does not forget her little quip: what did the kiddy die of? Neglect? The brutality of the exchange may be transparent to us, but even as she recounts it Irene remains convinced of her role as 'a public-spirited guardian of morals'.[29] More disturbingly, the violence and nastiness of the fiction she projects on the couple across the road comes from within – and it is no comfort in this respect that her best friend in prison turns out to be a child murderer. The fantasy she has generated is a product of a mind warped by barrenness, solitude, and lovelessness, and helps explain why she finds happiness only among the tortured souls she encounters in prison.

One of the most important lessons of Bennett's work is that the meanings we ascribe to the accidents of the world are more revealing of ourselves than of anyone else. In *The Insurance Man*, one of the Kafka plays, Kafka remarks that 'Accidents, as we well know, are never an accident.'[30] For Bennett, the need to ascribe meaning is pervasive and confining, and derives from a refusal to accept that chance events are meaningless. If he seems an unlikely subject for a Bennett play, it is worth recalling that as an insurance man Kafka spent virtually every day of his working life meeting the victims of accidents.

The Insurance Man follows a claimant, Franz, round the offices of the insurance company for which Kafka worked. As he discovers, all his fellow-claimants are in search of meaning. They pass through the corridors of the insurance building clutching files of information relating to their accidents. In one scene Franz encounters a young woman who tells him: 'Papers, facts, they all come into it, possibly. You've got to keep track.'[31] Later, her condition is explained by a Lecturer:

> A box fell on her head. She took a few days off and she felt none the worse. But then she heard that in this enlightened age there is compensation for those that suffer injury at work. . . . 'Is she entitled to this?' she wonders. And the wondering turns to worrying as she begins to lie awake at night suffering from headaches. She is increasingly unhappy. . . . And so begins her quest for compensation but for what? Not the injury, for she has scarcely suffered one. And she is not malingering for the headaches are real. And to those of you who say there is no injury therefore there can be no compensation she can say, 'But I was not like this before my accident. I had no quest. Looking for what is wrong with me *is* what is wrong with me!'[32]

The Lecturer is explaining a real condition. Like all accidents, the one that initiated Lily's neurosis was without significance. But, as Kafka observes, accidents are never accidental, and even though hers is not, at least directly, the cause of her present misery, it drives her to seek compensation. That search is accompanied by that for a cause. Franz himself is not immune from this in his quest for compensation for the skin disease he has contracted at work. 'What is it?' he shouts at the Lecturer, 'What have I done? Give me something. Give me something for it. Stop it. It's all over my body. Why? Why?' The ambiguity of his question takes us beyond the realms of physiology, and indicates that his affliction and the headaches which trouble Lily are symptomatic of a more than purely physical malaise. It's hardly coincidental that 'What have I done?' and 'Why?' are the very questions posed vainly by the protagonists of Kafka's novels. As one of the insurance company's doctors observes,

> We cannot compensate people for being cast out of Paradise. All these sheaves of reports are saying is 'I didn't know how lucky I was till this happened.' So? Now they do know. They have achieved wisdom. And a degree of self-knowledge. They should be paying us, not we them.[33]

This diagnosis may be correct, but it is also cruel. Paradise is invoked only so that it can be denied, while the consequences of accident are made their own reward. Worst of all, the doctor denies the very need that accident insurance is designed to encourage: resolution, redress, healing. Milton, famously, was unable to leave his public merely with *Paradise Lost*; they demanded that he compose *Paradise Regained*. If this is not adequate, if our myths are invoked only to mock us, perhaps it is best not to mythologise at all.

Rather than explore their seductive power, Bennett prefers in *The Insurance Man* to expose their self-deceiving purpose. If we detect brutality in the observation that 'We cannot compensate people for being cast out of Paradise', we may also find truth. Bennett's Kafka makes the same point, though in a gentler way, when he tells Franz that 'You are asking for a justice that doesn't exist in the world. And not only you. More people. More people every year.' Insurance is a fiction designed to give meaning to the random and the arbitrary. Franz tracks Kafka down because, as he says to him, 'I've been told you are kind. . . . They say you are a human being',[34] but the irony is that Kafka retains his humanity only so that he can testify to the inherently accidental nature of life and the futility of compensation. He argues his case by reference to an imaginary case of a millworker who falls ill from dust inhalation:

> No beam has fallen on his head. No bottle has exploded in his eye. He has not got his shirt caught in the shaft and been taken round. All that has happened is that he has been inhaling cotton dust for some years. And day by day this cotton dust has crept into his lungs, but so slowly, so gradually that it cannot be called an accident. But suppose our lungs were not internal organs. Suppose they were not locked away in the chest. Suppose we carried our lungs outside our bodies, bore them before us, could

hold and handle them, cradle them in our arms. And suppose further they were not made of flesh but of glass, or something like glass, not yet invented, something pliable. And thus the effect of each breath could be seen, the deposit of each intake of air, calculated, weighed even. What would we say then, as we saw the dust accumulate, the passages clog, the galleries close down, as cell by cell these lungs hardened, withered, died. . . . And if we were able to magnify each inhalation, see under the microscope each breath, capture the breath that killed the cell, register the gasp that caused the cough that broke the vein that atrophied the flesh. Wouldn't that be an accident? A very small accident?[35]

'People will be wanting compensation for being alive next', says one of Kafka's colleagues; his humane response is indicated in a stage direction: he 'looks as if this might not be a bad idea.' His speech is all the more poignant for its anticipation of his own death, precipitated by inhalation of asbestos. This irony is compounded in turn when he offers the unemployed Franz a job in the very factory where he himself was to inhale the deadly fibres. As the champion of 'a scrupulous and vigilant humanity',[36] he is the cause of the play's hardest irony, for the job leads ultimately to Franz's death from lung cancer. In the final scene of the play, Franz's doctor remarks: 'You weren't to know. He wasn't to know. You breathed, that's all you did wrong.'[37] These ironies are only emphasised by the randomness of these events. Kafka meets Franz by accident; only by accident is Kafka aware on that day of the opening of the asbestos factory because, by chance, its owner is his brother-in-law.

Accident is the essence of life; ubiquitous, ineluctable, meaningless. And yet, if the urge to ascribe meaning is confining, our submission to the very antithesis of meaning – accident – represents a kind of freedom. After all, accident can work in our favour as well as against it; it operates on us all, without prejudice, all the time.

Sydney, the protagonist of the second of the Kafka plays, *Kafka's Dick*, is also an insurance man. As he observes, this is not the only thing he has in common with his favourite writer:

He'd like me. We've got so much in common. He was in insurance. I'm in insurance. He had TB. I had TB. He didn't like his name. I don't like my name. I'm sure the only reason I drifted into insurance was because I was called Sydney.[38]

But this does not make Sydney another Kafka. If, as with all accidents of fate, these signify nothing, that should not blind us to the fact that they serve the same function as the moral constructs in other Bennett plays: they make life bearable. That existential nightmare, the chaos beneath the surface, the ruffian on the stair, is what really terrifies his characters. In this light Bennett's admiration for the plays of Joe Orton might be explained partly by an affinity,[39] for Orton's characters move in a world of which his often dream, in which moral imperatives are irrelevant. As John Lahr has written, 'Orton's plays wanted to defy gravity (in both senses of the word).'[40]

The only character in *Kafka's Dick* to experience weightlessness of this kind is Sydney's wife, Linda. When Kafka comes back from the dead, Sydney cannot help but encounter him in the context of what he has read, and ends up putting him on trial, summoning Kafka's parents as witnesses. Extreme though it may sound, this is the acting-out of a reflex we all share; as Sydney observes, 'writers are tried by readers every time they open their books.'[41] Not having read any books by or about him, Linda has no preconceptions about Kafka, and when he declares 'I am a terrible human being', she replies 'No. You're a man, that's all.'[42] Openly deplored by the male characters, this is nonetheless one of the most important speeches in the play, for it releases Kafka from the fiction supported by Sydney's random facts. Bennett first articulated that fiction in a short sketch broadcast by the BBC in 1976 in which he satirised the attitudes of those who make arts documentaries: 'Art is pain. It must be. Or it isn't fair.'[43] Put another way, if some of us are to be literary geniuses, they had better pay for it. The myth of art as suffering is another attempt to give meaning to the accident by which talent is doled out in unequal measure. In this cause the magnifying glass of the biographer lends a disproportionate and bogus significance to every fact relating to its subject. As Linda complains, 'I know W. H. Auden never wore underpants, that Kafka's grandfather could pick up a sack of potatoes in his teeth and that Kafka's father used to rummage in his ears with a toothpick. Because that kind of conversation is all I ever get.'[44] This reaches an extreme when Sydney shows Linda a book 'by two psychologists at the University of North Carolina, who having analysed everything Kafka ever wrote, deduce that one of his problems, of which there were many, was a small penis'.[45] If, compared with the arguments of many academics, this seems an unexceptional thesis, it nevertheless retains a charming absurdity. Which is, of course, the point: Kafka is not being mocked, we are. Our expectation as critics, biographers, readers, is that writers must pay for their greatness, however absurd the means of payment. That mythological transaction has no more bearing on reality than the moral judgements made of Anthony Blunt and Guy Burgess; all it does is reflect our hunger for meaning – the very need that provides the subject of Kafka's novels and stories. As Sydney remarks,

SYDNEY: Gossip is the acceptable face of intellect.

LINDA: What I don't understand, she said, like the secretary in the detective story when the loose ends are being tied up, what I still don't understand is why people are so interested in a writer's life in the first place.

SYDNEY: You like fairy stories.

LINDA: If they have happy endings.

SYDNEY: This one does, every, every time. We are reading a book. A novel, say, or a book of short stories. It interests us because it is new, because it is . . . novel, so we read on. And yet in what we call our heart of hearts (which is the part that is heartless) we know that like children we prefer the familiar stories, the tales we have been told before. And there is one story we never fail to like because it is always the same. The myth of the artist's life.

How one struggled for years against poverty and indifference only to die and find himself famous. Another is a prodigy finding his way straight to the public's heart to be loved and celebrated while still young, but paying the price by dying and being forgotten. Or just dying.

This one is a hermit, that one a hellraiser but the myth can accommodate them all, no variation on it but it is familiar even to someone who has never read a book. He plunges from a bridge and she hits the bottle. Both of them *paid*. That is the myth. Art is not a gift, it is a transaction, and somewhere an account has to be settled. It may be in the gas oven, in front of a train or even at the altar but on this side of the grave or that settled it must be. We like to be told, you see, that you can't win. We prefer artists to die poor and forgotten, like Rembrandt, Mozart or Beethoven, none of

whom did, quite. One reason why Kafka is so celebrated is
because his life conforms in every particular to what we have
convinced ourselves an artist's life should be. Destined to
write he dispenses with love, with fame and finally with life
itself so that it seems at the last he has utterly failed.[46]

As an aspirant biographer himself Sydney has thrown in his lot with
the mythologists, including the shop assistant in *An Englishman
Abroad* and Irene in *A Lady of Letters*, who employ an unfeeling
morality to drag the spirit down to earth; he even admits that 'I just
want to cut him down to size. If I do that I might make my name.'[47]
Blissful ignorance is also, in this context, innocence, for it is against
this fictionalising impulse that Linda tells Kafka, 'You're a man,
because, although you despair, at the same time like all men you
believe your despair is important. You think you're insignificant but
your insignificance is not insignificant.'[48] Where the myths go
wrong is in sniffing out difference, when in fact the urge to create
springs from shared experience: namely, insignificance and despair.
   But myths depend on the extraordinary, and facts such as the
dimensions of Kafka's dick serve only to obscure a deeper truth –
that an artist's aspirations are ordinary and mundane, like our own.
The clarity of vision that enables Linda to recognise and articulate
this is as subversive as anything in Orton. And as in Orton, the
clearest view is that which transcends the defensive reflexes of
morality and prejudice, and acknowledges the innate anarchy of the
human spirit. He may be no utopian, but Bennett's dedication to
such metaphysical notions, however reluctantly declared, reveals an
idealistic streak that makes his one of the most humane voices in
contemporary theatre. The relation of all this to *Kafka's Dick* is
encapsulated by Auden in a poem composed in 1934, and inspired
apparently by Liddell Hart's biography of T. E. Lawrence.

   A shilling life will give you all the facts:
   How Father beat him, how he ran away,
   What were the struggles of his youth, what acts
   Made him the greatest figure of his day:
   Of how he fought, fished, hunted, worked all night,
   Though giddy, climbed new mountains; named a sea:
   Some of the last researchers even write
   Love made him weep his pints like you and me.

With all his honours on, he sighed for one
Who, say astonished critics, lived at home;
Did little jobs about the house with skill
And nothing else; could whistle; would sit still
Or potter round the garden; answered some
Of his long marvellous letters but kept none.[49]

3

Dennis Potter:
The Angel in Us

In Dennis Potter's 1972 television play, *Follow the Yellow Brick Road*, a doctor asks Jack Black, an actor, if he still believes in God.

For years and years I hadn't thought about it, hadn't considered it. I just – assumed – somehow – that he – it – was – there, still there, still watching, still *present* – Then – then . . . Then one morning – daybreak – I – well, I'd been up all night. Couldn't think. Couldn't sleep. Couldn't sit. Couldn't stand. She – (*Abrupt change.*) I was alone. I could see light in a chink through the curtains. First light. Half-past four in the morning and – Oh, birds. They were singing. Mad chatter of them. A dog was barking, somewhere across acres of concrete. Empty yearning. First light. First sounds of the day. (*Bitter laugh.*) New Every Morning. I thought – I stopped in the middle of the room – I thought it's been *like this* since the world began. Light pushing back dark. Birds jabbering. New day starting. What for? What *for*? So – so I tried to – for the first time in years and years I – it seemed – (*Rush.*) I got down on my knees and I closed my eyes and I put my hands together and I said to myself I won't ask for anything, won't ask, *won't ask*, not even for . . . (*Stop.*) I'll just let *you* come. I'll just see if you are there if you are still there still there – I'll wait. I'll wait for – (*Gets it out.*) – *the word*.
(*Silence. He works his face, remembering it, reliving it. . .*)
I waited. I waited and waited. I just wanted the word to drop into my mind. I was open for it. *Ready* for it. In my mind I got off my tricycle again and ran to the side, ran to the grass bank – (*He stops. . .*)
Slime!. . . That was the word! Slime. That was the message I got. No God. On my knees with my eyes shut I got this one word or feeling or impression or – I don't know – but there it was, long slippery strands of it – slime, nothing else but slime. (*Chokes.*) And

dirt and – stinking slime contaminating everything. All over my
hands. All over my face. In my mouth. In my eyes. . . . I was
kneeling in a s – a s – in a s – in a sewer . . . lumps of . . . swirling
all over all over all over . . . everything. (*He puts his hand to his
mouth, retching.*)[1]

No wonder Potter's audience has had such a hard time swallowing
what he has to say. Even his best work is permeated by a crazed,
visceral loathing of physical process. It is unsettling to encounter a
television writer so intent on exposing our least attractive frailties to
public view – though it may be partly for that very reason that he
comes closer than anyone else in the medium to realising Artaud's
demand for a drama that 'must present everything in love, crime,
war and madness'.[2] (Artaud, however, would have hated the idea of
televised drama.)

Jack Black's intoxicated expressions of disgust are significant
because they expose not despair but the vacuum left by the absence
of belief. Potter admits that in *Follow the Yellow Brick Road* 'I wanted,
half mockingly, and with an extremely grudging acknowledgement
of what I was myself beginning to understand, to show how the
human dream will surface and take hold of whatever circumstances
are at hand – no matter how ludicrous.'[3] In Jack Black's case the
human dream assumes control, in his imagination, of the world of
the television commercials in which he appears:

> They have happy families in the commercials. Husbands and
> wives who *love* each other. . . . There's laughter and, and, and
> sunshine and kids playing in the meadows. Nobody mocks the
> finest human aspirations. There's no deliberate wallowing in vice
> and evil and and (*Breaks off.*) No. There's nothing wrong with the
> commercials. Nothing at all![4]

Given his way, Jack would translate himself permanently into the
trailers for Krispy Krunch biscuits and Waggytail Din-Din by which
the play is punctuated. But the secular nature of those paradisal
interludes signals his desperation; even before the play begins he
has relinquished the ideal of which television advertisements are a
hideous parody. When he prays to God, he hears only 'Slime!. . .
That was the word! Slime. That was the message I got. No God.'
God's failure to exist is irritating enough, but Jack's rage feeds not
on this alone. In an interview in 1978, Potter observed that

the shape of our lives belongs to what I falteringly think of (there is no way to say this word in a modern context except in quotes) as God. It is the one thing which separates us from the entire universe and whether we're tasting a squashy plum or crunchy cornflakes, there is something so utterly unique about being oneself which cannot be translated into any other terms except that sense of a rational, loving order of life. Which is, I suppose, why I have a basically religious sense of the universe.[5]

Admitted only in quotation marks, God is a concept from which Potter retreats, preferring the vaguer 'sense of a rational, loving order of life' and 'a basically religious sense of the universe'. Arising from the unique experience of being oneself, these perceptions are the end result of an essentially psychological process.

In other words, Potter's is a declaration less of faith than need. We may kill God but the *need* to believe in him lives on. So it is that Philip Marlow, the pulp novelist in *The Singing Detective*, confesses to his psychiatrist that 'I would have liked to have used my pen to praise a loving God and all his loving creation.'[6] Potter's protagonists may be fated to share their creator's 'religious sense of the universe', but for none of them can it be satisfied. Having collapsed, the beliefs that once sustained now betray them to the filth and slime of the physical world. This is true even of Christ in *Son of Man*, Potter's retelling of the gospels, who declares:

The son of man must be a man. He must be all of a man. He must pass water like a man. . . . He cannot be other than a man, or else God has *cheated*. . . . And so my Father in Heaven will abandon me to myself. And if my head aches he will not lift the ache out of it. And if my stomach rumbles he will not clean out my bowels. And if a snake curls into my thoughts, then the fang will be in my mind. If I were to have *no* doubt I would be *other than a man*.[7]

Potter's Christ is a madman from the desert, filthy and crazed, bereft of the divine gifts and visitations described in the Bible. In fact, Potter's version of this story displaces the miraculous in favour of the rebarbative, so that in one scene Christ is said to be 'talking to God' when he is actually being sick. The gap between ideal and the fallen world leads to the ultimate betrayal when Christ dies forsaken; significantly, Potter chooses to end his play with the crucifixion, implicitly casting doubt over the events that followed.

Where Christ is doomed to accept his abandonment, other Potter characters fight it. For Jack Black, betrayal leads to frustration, and his expressions of horror and loathing never lose their tone of moral outrage – as he exclaims at one point: 'Barnes Common is full of used contraceptives. Dribbling out rancid juice on the poisoned grass!'[8]

Follow the Yellow Brick Road is remarkable not least because it represents a triumph of content over form. Few writers could have pulled off a play so consumed by its own bile. Like *Son of Man*, it questions insistently, urgently, and fails to find answers. In this respect there is a curiously bathetic quality to the early dramas, as if they are in some crucial respect unfinished. This is less true of *Brimstone and Treacle* (1976), essentially a fable about a paraplegic girl, Pattie, whose life revolves entirely around physical need.

Over the sandwich his wife has made for dinner, her father, Mr Bates, imagines what her condition must be like if she is conscious.

> It's like having an anaesthetic and you are lying there completely paralysed so far as everyone else is concerned. They think you are out, right out. But all the time you can hear what they are saying. All the time you can see the sharp – the shiny – weapon in the surgeon's meaty hand and – and – no matter what they do to you or how much it hurts there is no way you can stop them, no way of letting them know that you are not unconscious . . . . I don't want this. I don't want to eat this.[9]

If God is the surgeon, we are the patients – betrayed, as thinking, conscious beings, into old age, sickness, and death. The resentment and nausea that inform this speech indicate Mr Bates' kinship with Jack Black. Even the inability to eat his sandwich arises less out of disappointment at the absence of a proper meal than out of loathing of the human condition. When Mrs Bates suggests some cheese and an apple he responds: 'I don't want to eat. I can't swallow it.'[10] His refusals confirm him as the sceptic of the family, and at one point he rebukes his wife with the declaration that 'There is no God. There are no miracles. Stop hoping for what can never, ever be.'[11] He rejects out of hand his wife's religious conviction which leads her to see in her daughter's eyes 'a different sort of expression': 'There's a light in her eyes. From inside, I mean. A definite light. . . . A definite *human* light. As though something deep inside her is trying to come back to us.'[12]

These opposing convictions are in some sense resolved by Martin, a young man claiming to be a former friend of Pattie's. Having tricked her parents into allowing him to stay, he rapes Pattie while Mrs Bates is doing the shopping. Immediately before she leaves the house, Martin tells her: 'You have to be able to choose between good and evil, you see. And for that, you have to have a soul.'[13] His irony may be directed at Mrs Bates, whose trust is admittedly misplaced, but it rebounds against him, for he fails to foresee that his assault of Pattie will, in the play's last moments, lead to her recovery. *Brimstone and Treacle* is a celebration of moral confusion; as Potter puts it: 'There is, in the end, no such thing as a *simple* faith, and we cannot even begin to define "good" and "evil" without being aware of the interaction between the two.'[14]

Pattie's last-minute recovery comes within a hair's breadth of melodrama because it aims to revalue what Jack Black called 'the finest human aspirations' in a world in which a beautiful young girl can be turned into a paraplegic by a hit and run driver. Only a playwright as sensitive as Potter to visionary and moral loss would set himself such a challenge. That sensibility bears directly on the psychological realms which his characters inhabit and, as he recalls in the Preface to his collection of television plays, *Waiting for the Boat*, owes much to events in his own childhood:

> I don't know whether it was too obvious 'cleverness', examination salted, which ensured my early isolation, or whether, as I now dare to think but not inspect, something foul and terrible that happened to me when I was 10 years old, caught by an adult's appetite and abused out of innocence. But certainly, and with a kind of cunning shame, I grew for long into someone too wary, too cut off, too introspective, too reclusive, until, finally, as though out of the blue, or the black, too ill to function properly.
>
> Perhaps we all live in a sort of exile from the lost land of childhood. Not in the futile second-order emotion of mere nostalgia, nor with the lacerations of an even worse and even more futile remorse, and certainly with no heedless sentimentality. But simply, and impossibly, with the desire that we could stand where the earth once sang with magic, and look at ourselves as we are now.[15]

Intimations of abuse, followed by a rapid descent from grace, haunt almost all of Potter's protagonists, culminating in rages inspired by frustration and denial. But what vexes and disturbs most is the knowledge of loss; as Wordsworth put it, 'Whither is fled the visionary gleam?/ Where is it now, the glory and the dream?'

The turning-point in Potter's career came with *Pennies From Heaven* (1978): where the plays preceding it were distinguished by an intense anger arising from disappointment and betrayal, *Pennies* goes one step further to reveal how that pain might be resolved. That crucial development in his thinking gave rise to his most accomplished television serial to date – one containing the seeds of nearly all the television writing he has subsequently produced. As the screenplay remains unpublished, my quotations are taken from his novel of the same name, an underrated work which brings us much closer to his aims than the film on which it is based.[16] Like the film, the novel is set in America – mainly Chicago – in 1934; the television version was set in the Forest of Dean and London.

Arthur Parker, the sheet music salesman of *Pennies*, is one of Potter's simplest protagonists, characterised by his unquestioning belief in the 1930s dance tunes he peddles. 'They tell the truth, songs do',[17] he tells Al and Ed, the travelling salesmen he meets in a roadside diner:

'Years and years I didn't really know what I was selling,' he said. 'The songs! What they are all about! The way they *do* – *really* do – tell the truth, the honest-to-God truth. And they do! They do! Goddamn it, they do!'

'What? Them songs?' protested Ed, incredulous. Them silly toons? Molasses in the moonlight. Horse-shit under the stars!

Al didn't say anything. He couldn't. His mouth was locked open.

'Somewhere the sun *is* shining,' Arthur insisted, brushing aside the dirt that had fouled up his vision. 'And do you know where? Inside! Inside yourself. Inside your own head – in the spaces in between! That's where the blue and the gold is. On the other side of the black! I learned that last night.'

'Ah – aaaah!' said Ed and Al, in unison again.

It was perfectly clear, once more, what had happened to good ol' Arthur last night. He was simply letting himself be carried away by what must have been an exceptionally enjoyable lay. They exchanged complicit sniggers.[18]

Popular music such as 'The Clouds Will Soon Roll By', to which Arthur alludes, is to him what commercials were to Jack Black. But Arthur lacks the wit to deconstruct the impossible dreams they inspire. At one point Potter describes the historical period in which his story is set as 'the middle of the dishonest 1930s'[19] – alerting us to Arthur's besetting sin. He is too wrapped up in fantasy to confront the horse-shit under the stars, or the possibility that his optimism may indeed be connected with the affair he is having with Eileen.

In the BBC serial, musical interludes arose directly out of Arthur's deceived imagination, expressing the unrealistic aspirations that he had appropriated. They are products of his own delusions – or, as Potter remarks, 'genuine artefacts from the past that had been cannibalized and transformed into the workings of the head. If the characters had genuinely sung them it would have been a musical.'[20] In the novel, he is even clearer:

> *Songs tell the truth, songs do.*
>
> No: they probably don't, unless by The Truth you mean some tiny, glistening sliver of it, a fragment of broken glass in the long grass of our overgrown experience. A jagged piece of waste which fleetingly, and mockingly, catches and refracts the rays of the sun.[21]

The word 'mockingly' is all-important. Mimed by Arthur, the songs operate ironically. He believes in their corny, second-order ideals at his own expense: the central character in a parable in which a man who believes that pennies rain from heaven ends up being hanged for a crime he didn't commit. Songs bear only a tangential relation to truth, catching and *refracting* the sun's rays.

Arthur's self-deception is sustained by his ability to repress. The voracity of the feeding pigs on Eileen's farm is described as 'so splendidly uninhibited that it had the power to shake up the sense of appetite in a human onlooker'.[22] Like Eileen, they are in direct contact with their feelings and urges. Arthur lacks any such honesty, and shares with his wife Joan a prudishness about sex. He accuses his colleagues Al and Ed of being 'dirty', 'filthy',[23] and asks Eileen 'Haven't you got any shame?'[24] after she is forced to become a prostitute. But his moral scruples are empty and unfounded. In fact, he lacks the sensitivity to realise how appalling are the sexual demands he makes on his wife: 'Arthur had little idea of how much, in her order of things, he was abusing her. Nor could he admit to the buried or subdued rage which was in him as he demanded more and more energetic sexual callisthenics from her.'[25] His moral blindness reveals a sinister side to his character, developed in the more malign Uncle Kingsley of *Blackeyes*. As for Joan, she is even more repressed than Arthur, and, believing him to be a monster and a pervert, is imagined 'holding sharp scissors in her hand'.[26]

Arthur confesses to Joan that one of his dearest wishes is to play the saxophone. If it leads her to doubt his sanity,[27] it also takes us to the roots of his psychology:

> When Arthur was much younger he had heard a saxophone sending out its sobbing blue rhythms as he stood buying a ticket at the entrance to a small Chicago dance-hall. The music had been distanced by a wall and a pair of glass doors, and there were boys and girls milling about in the foyer. The boys hunted in packs, and the girls were in pairs. Jaws moved chewing-gum about drying mouths, and eyes whisked around the wall, too afraid to settle. The music from the makeshift band from within had the wistful suggestion of present and future loneliness. It seemed, to the young people who heard it, to be trying to say something important. Find what you want or who you desire *now*, or be lost for ever. Crack your jokes, put on your style, curl your lip, but don't hang about on the edge of the floor . . . it will go, it will be gone, and the shine on the apple will dull and then rot, and your limbs will stiffen and decay, and the music will cease to play.[28]

One of the moral lessons of *Pennies* is that maturity consists in accommodating loss within our psychological economy. Only when we have accepted our fallen nature can we assume the adult obligations which we owe ourselves and others. Arthur's failure to do this has made him faithless, self-serving, blind and desperate – qualities that explain why he married Joan, to whom he is unsuited. Left to his own devices, Arthur learns nothing, enslaved to ideals that continue to elude him and that foster his dishonesty. Nor does his basic insecurity enable him to manage his emotions. The most striking example of this occurs when first he sees the blind girl for whose murder he will later be executed:

> Arthur watched her go, and the sight of her made his eyes prickle. As ever, he was a man easily moved.
>
> 'I'd cut off my right arm if I could make you see again,' he said out loud, but far too quietly for her to hear. 'I don't know what I'd do if I could – if I could . . .'
>
> Alas, his expression changed.
>
> 'If I could get into your pants,' he added, *definitely* to himself.[29]

The incident dramatises Arthur's basic confusion. Being repressed, he cannot extricate such virtuous wishes as that to restore her sight from his sexual desires. As Potter remarks of the episode: 'His instant emotion was there, and then that sexuality was there. He couldn't deal with his emotions at all. There are lots of people like that.'[30] That basic confusion makes Arthur doubt his innocence when he hears that he is the chief suspect in the girl's murder. Appropriately, his *doppelgänger*, the nameless accordion-player who is guilty, suffers a similar confusion, and a similarly repressed understanding of his sexual nature, as he reflects on his crime: 'But when after a while he saw what he had done, when the sticky fervour had gone off the part of his own flesh that also belonged to the same Devil who had put her eyes out, he wept in despair.'[31]

However, *Pennies From Heaven* is distinct from the dramas that precede it in that it is essentially comic, and Arthur is, ultimately, redeemed. He is guided out of hell by Eileen, whose chief virtue is that she is unrepressed, completely in touch with her feelings and appetites:

> Arthur already knew that she had a steadier resolve than he had ever been able to aspire to, let alone emulate. He knew that she did not shift her eyes about when she wanted to know something, whether it was painful or not. For all her shy hesitancy there was a directness and an honesty about her which, at times, was only the finest slither away from hardness.[32]

Eileen is the closest Potter ever comes to describing an ideal woman. Her attraction lies not in physical beauty, but in her self-possession. When Arthur abandons her she gets an abortion and becomes a prostitute in order to survive, but without any of the self-deception to which he is prone. And she is, for this reason, a much more substantial character.

In the novel, Potter's most audacious trick – one denied to viewers of the television or film versions – is to step outside the narrative for a moment and address us directly. Chapter 26, he tells us, is 'a hole in the narrative while Eileen Everson sells her body on the streets of Chicago':[33]

> There is no need – and, in any case, no probability – of describing 'all out' this section of Eileen's biography. It was a series of sordid encounters and degraded copulations, where she

counted the money first, a dollar at a time. It was a descent into the nether land of the flesh, where all that is not tinted is irredeemably tainted.

And yet it did not seem to touch her.

This is why there is a hole in the narrative, and why the chapter is not a chapter. There is no possibility of representing the manner in which it is true to assert that what she did, day upon day or night upon night, had no effect upon her.[34]

So real is she, that some part of Eileen's personality remains impenetrable and mysterious. That sense of a unique and unknowable self – a self inaccessible even to the probing eye of the narrator – underlies her psychological reality. It is a quality that neither Arthur nor Joan ever acquire, Arthur because he is too simple, Joan because we never explore her world in detail. It is passed on to all the major protagonists in Potter's subsequent work – Marlow in *The Singing Detective* and Jessica in *Blackeyes*. Endowed with a strength Arthur lacks, Eileen teaches him a crucial moral lesson as they are on the run from the police. Arthur is terrified at the prospect of being executed for the blind girl's murder. 'Don't you love me?' he asks her, as she walks away from him. 'Not when you are so scared', she replies:

> She put it in the simplest terms possible.
> 'We've only got one life, Arthur,' she said, matter-of-fact. 'We both know we've made a mess of ours. It doesn't seem to matter much how it ends. Does it?'
> Arthur was puzzled, and he was scared. The bleak implacability of the proposition was against his nature. He was a child in this, forever wanting to be assured that there was always icing on the cake, and cherries on the bough.
> 'Doesn't it?' he asked, numbly.
> Eileen waited. She let him stare at her.
> 'No', she said.
> Arthur took it all in, her word, her expression. He saw with relief how hard and strong she was.[35]

This is the most important scene in the drama, as it signals a fundamental alteration in Arthur's personality. For the first time, he is compelled to understand someone else's feelings, and is changed by them. His relief at Eileen's strength enables him to be strong too, so that when he is arrested, he protests his innocence only once, and then, 'with a determination rare to him, he decided that he was not going to say another word. They were taking him away from Eileen, and he was not going to speak until they could be joined again.'[36] This is the moral core of the drama. With the assumption of a new-found self-assurance, Arthur values his love for Eileen fully for the first time; it is, nevertheless, an insight that cannot change the outcome of the trial.

Had the television serial concluded with Arthur's execution it would have mimicked the tragic structure of *King Lear*, but Potter added a coda in which Arthur was resurrected and reunited with Eileen on Hammersmith Bridge.[37] The novel too carries an important epilogue:

> Arthur and Eileen are embracing. So tenderly. So lovingly.
> 'We couldn't go through all that without a happy ending,' he is saying. 'Songs ain't like that! Are they?' Well, they are not, are they?
> They both turn, and they are looking at you. If you want them to.
> 'The song is ended,' they say. 'But the melody lingers on.'
> And from all around, the music is playing. Arthur and Eileen are singing.
> The Glory of Love.
> The world was through with them, but they still, it seems, had each other's arms. In a brilliant sky, cavernous, clear and endless. A space in the head.[38]

At the beginning of the story, the songs were all the reality Arthur had; the epilogue revalues their aspirations in the light of the moral lesson he has learnt. They do have something important to tell us, but only in the context of a world – and a self – with which we have come to terms. There *is* another way of seeing – reality *can* be punctured – but only if you are not deceiving yourself about the nature of that reality.

Arthur's moral failings are amplified in Bernard, the repressed, dull protagonist of *Cream in my Coffee* (1979), who defies his possessive mother and proposes marriage to his girlfriend Jean, who he knows to be less than the witty, beautiful woman he desires. Such impetuousness results in a lifetime of misery, for Jean can no more live up to his expectations than he can sustain the romantic promise

of his proposal. Hours before his death in old age, he tells Jean about
'An old witch and her mangy old tom-cat' who lived nearby during
his childhood.

> BERNARD: I saw her one morning. I shall never forget it, not as
> long as I live. She had come out as far as the broken-down old
> wall, looking for the cat. Then I saw her pick up this stiff dead
> thing from the long grass. It was the cat. Must have been
> dead for days.
> JEAN: Oh, dear.
> BERNARD: And do you know what she did? She kissed it and
> hugged it and kissed it. On the mouth, mind you. On its
> stinking mouth. Crying and wailing all the time.
> JEAN: How horrible.
> BERNARD: And then she suddenly tossed it aside. Threw it
> away. She stopped crying and kissing it and just threw it
> down in the grass like a sack of potatoes. And went back to
> the house as though nothing whatsoever had happened. I
> don't know why it made such a profound impression on me,
> but it did.[39]

Devoid of the illusion that has destroyed Bernard's life with Jean,
the old lady's love of her cat is as unintellected and impulsive as
childhood emotion. And because it transcends the corporeal she is
able to fling its bodily remains 'in the grass like a sack of potatoes'. It
is a vision of an ideal love. Bernard has related a parable the
morality of which he does not understand, though it bears directly
on his own life. Blind to metaphysics, he fails to see how his
deceived notions of Jean have destroyed his affection for her and led
to bitterness, and at the end of the play has a heart attack while
beating her about the head with a cocktail menu – a bleakly
appropriate emblem of his thwarted expectations and misdirected
anger. Unlike Arthur, Bernard goes unredeemed.

Refusing to settle for the barely continent fury of Potter's early
work, *Cream in my Coffee* builds on the insights of *Pennies From
Heaven*. By the late 1970s he was searching for ways of reconciling
the 'human dream' with the material world. Middle-aged, thwarted,
nostalgic, Jack Barker, the hero of his 1983 stage play, *Sufficient
Carbohydrate*, fits the character profile of Potter's protagonists
exactly. So disgusted is he with the American conglomerate that
has taken over his food factory that he goes round the offices

screaming and kicking the radiators.[40] When Eddie, an American colleague, takes him on holiday to force him into line at the company's request, Jack discovers that Eddie is having an affair with his wife.

Disgust at marital infidelity is merely the symptom of a deeper pathology; as Eddie's son Clayton puts it, 'You're dirty! All of you! Dirty!' The association of physical filth with moral failure leads Jack to tell Eddie that 'We're missing a trick in the food-processing business':

JACK: Instead of using dipotassium phosphate and sodium caseinate to replace milk in coffee and extra microbes to help *whippability* we ought to add blood and nerve tissue to our hamburgers. Human blood. Human tissue. Adequate protein. Sufficient carbohydrate.

EDDIE: What are you talking about?

JACK: People like to eat all sorts of things, Eddie, from snails to bullocks' testicles. But what they really want, what people really want to get between their teeth and slowly chew and swallow is other people. People want to eat people. They dribble at the mouth at the very thought of it. Have *you* got wet lips, Eddie? And blood on your teeth – eh?[41]

Chewing, swallowing, dribbling, the humans in Jack's world are no better than the animals they eat. Although this line of attack is familiar from earlier plays, in 1983 it seemed more than usually pertinent; after all, sufficient carbohydrate is not just a sales ploy but a potent metaphor for the unquestioning amorality of Mrs Thatcher's enterprise culture, a world in which dog eats dog. This brings us very close to the kind of insight offered by Shakespearean tragedy, in which, as I suggested in the Introduction,[42] human love is shown to be impotent against the injustice of the outside world.

If Potter does not develop his political subtext[43] – and he has never been as forthrightly ideological as, say, Howard Brenton or David Hare – Jack is nevertheless the first of his protagonists to outgrow an entrenched indignation generated partly by the effects of enterprise culture. Having observed that melancholy is 'an act of mental hygiene',[44] he applies the undeceived vision of the old witch to human nature, and concludes, in conversation with Clayton, that life is a sea voyage undertaken with other people who 'feel lost at times. . . . We can't help it. It's the nature of the vessel, old son. And the peril of the journey.'[45] The retreat from idealism implied by Jack's acceptance of the flaws in our moral fabric is only partial, for at the conclusion of the play Clayton and Jack embrace 'in a sudden, compulsive, fragile humanity',[46] an image of emotional interdependence that underlines the affirmative impulses behind Potter's work. A similar embrace occurs in *Lipstick on Your Collar* (1993), when Aunt Vickie comforts her enemy, Sylvia, after her husband's death.[47]

The epic scale of *The Singing Detective* (1987) helped Potter set out his arguments in detail. He told the *New Musical Express* that it was 'about a man who doesn't know how to get better mentally, who is alienated and isolated, doesn't hope for anything, doesn't believe in anything. All his desires come down to his desire for the next cigarette.'[48] The extent of Marlow's alienation is as evident in his psoriatic arthropathy as in his nihilistic reworking of Jack Barker's metaphor: 'The captain is asleep. We are drifting off unanchored into the dark. We are lost. All of us. Lost.'[49] Marlow's novel, also called *The Singing Detective*, traces moral disillusionment to the act of conception:

> Mouth sucking wet and slack at mouth, tongue chafing against tongue, limb thrusting upon limb, skin rubbing at skin. Faces contort and stretch into a helpless leer, organs spurt out smelly stains and sticky betrayals. This is the sweaty farce out of which we are brought into being. We are implicated without choice in the slippery catastrophe of the copulations which splatter us into existence. We are spat out of fevered loins. We are the by-blows of grunts and pantings in a rumpled and creaking bed. Welcome.[50]

Where sexual disgust led Jacobean villains such as Flamineo and Iago to heights of entrepreneurial excess, taking outrageous risks for personal advancement, pimping their sisters to Dukes and so forth, it has the opposite effect on Potter's characters, who develop a morbid introspection which results in sickness and paralysis. In 1978 Potter recalled that during his own encounter with psoriatic arthropathy, he felt that 'the only meaningful sacrament left to human beings was for them to gather in the streets in order to be sick together, splashing vomit on the paving stones as the final and most eloquent plea to an apparently deaf, dumb and blind God.'[51] Religious ceremony is invoked for parodic purposes only; to congregate in an act of collective sickness would not only be futile, it would also be to deny the spiritual grace which the sacrament is intended to confirm. In the misery of our soiled, fallen state, a sense of the divine is burdensome.

'What do you live by?' one of the doctors asks Marlow. In a parody of the creed, he proclaims his belief in depopulation by means of 'cholesterol, cigarettes, alcohol, masturbation, carbon monoxide, the Arts Council, nuclear weapons, the *Daily Telegraph*, and not properly labelling fatal poisons. But most of all, above all else, I believe in the one thing which can come out of people's mouths. Vomit.'[52] In Marlow's hierarchy sick supplants speech, for words, as he tells Dr Gibbon, are 'where all the troubles of the world spring from'.[53] Only in the regurgitated images of the past, scrambled though they may be with the events of the present, can Marlow trail his sickness to its source. As we suspected all along, the crime and its detection are psychological. Not until Episode Three of the six-part serial is the initial 'crime' revealed. Unseen, the nine-year old Philip follows his mother and Raymond, a man from the village, through the woods, and witnesses their love-making:

> Mrs Marlow is flat on her back. The skirt of her thin and flowered dress is pulled up to her waist. Her legs are apart. Her heels are digging into the soft ground. And Raymond, his bare backside more visible than his face, grunts and labours on top of her, his trousers down around his ankles. . . . The strange sounds from the lovers make Philip stop, dead still, hardly daring to breathe. He looks, and he looks – and he looks. From the boy's incredulous point-of-view, the love-making seems akin to violence, or physical attack. Mrs Marlow's legs have tightened in a fierce clench, and she begins to cry out, uninhibitedly.[54]

'How did the Devil come? When first attack?' Such lurid episodes may not have been in Betjeman's mind when he composed *Norfolk*, the most elegiac of his poems on childhood, but the idea of a demonic assault on innocence fits well here. Young Philip can hardly be blamed for mistaking an act of love for one of violence, nor for his guilt at failing to intervene. When, partly as a result of her infidelity, his mother leaves his father and takes Philip back to London, his guilt finds expression in his thoughts: 'My fault. Me. It's me. Me. It's all my doing. Me. It's me. My fault. Mine. Our Father which art in heaven Hallow'd be Thy name . . .'[55] The process of introspective self-blame is already beginning, and will intensify when he discovers that the God he has been taught to love will neither absolve him nor reconcile his parents' differences. Words, once again, fail him. Words are the vehicle of betrayal.

Shortly after they arrive in London, Philip tells his mother what he saw and, unable to live with what she has done, she drowns herself in the Thames. This supremely self-repressive act triggers a similar response in Philip. He returns to live with his father in the country, but cannot tell him about his mother's infidelity, or the background to her death. 'Don't trust anybody again!' he says to himself, hiding from his father in the upper branches of a tree. 'Don't give your love. Hide in yourself. Or else they'll die. They'll die. And they'll hurt you! Hide! Hide!'[56] Believing his love to be poisoned, his emotional survival depends on retreat, tactics that make him antisocial and vindictive. As Potter has remarked of his own childhood trauma: 'It did affect me deeply. In adolescence, there were feelings of anxiety because it's the child that assumes guilt.'[57]

On returning to school Philip deliberately compounds his guilt by shitting on his teacher's table at school and blaming Raymond's son, letting him in for a beating from the headmaster. Years later, when he returns home, he hears that 'Mark is in the loony bin. . . . Been there for years. A complete nutter.'[58] By stifling his capacity to love, Philip has released destructive forces which both cause the disgust and hatred that sours his adult life, and intensify the guilt that leads to his disfiguring, crippling illness. As one of the patients in hospital says to him: 'I'll bet you lie there all day long thinking of *murdering* people – eh?'[59]

Crime detection is an apt metaphor for the psychoanalytic process leading to his recovery. In Marlow's novel the singing detective tracks down the murderer of a drowned woman. One of his fellow patients, Reginald, is reading it, and asks him to answer the question that provides its driving force: 'Who killed her. Who put her in the river. That girl.' Reginald cannot realise that his question takes us to the heart of Marlow's psychology. 'A swine', Marlow answers – with, the stage directions indicate, 'just a little too much feeling'.[60] That emotional blip hints at his hatred of the culprit who went into hiding long before the novel was written. 'Chronic illness is an extremely good shelter', Gibbon tells Marlow, underlining the fugitive nature of his emotions.[61] Nicola, Marlow's former wife, puts it differently: 'You're rotten with your own bile! You think you're smart but really you're very very sad, because you use your illness as a weapon against other people and as an excuse for not being properly human.'[62]

Marlow acknowledges his guilt only after confessing to Gibbon his framing of Raymond's son at school, admitting that 'We all have blood on our teeth.'[63] Before learning to be properly human we must first accept the flaws in the fabric. 'We are none of us good enough for this earth', says the preacher in *Joe's Ark* (1974), 'We all of us lack the holy imagination that could see life as the thrilling wondrous gift that it really is.'[64] Such insights are double-edged; sinful we may be, but recognition ought to promise more than repression. When Marlow's fellow-patient, Reginald, admits to being a former burglar, the man in the adjacent bed, Mr Hall, asks himself, in appalled tones, 'Who have I been next to all this time? What sort of person – ?' 'A *human* person', Reginald tells him.[65] The emphasis on humanity carries a revelatory power, for Marlow's denial of emotional truth has turned him, literally, into an unfeeling monster. Only by confronting the past can he slough off the self-protective scale of cynicism by which he is isolated; only then does he see that 'I didn't kill my Mum. It wasn't my doing.'[66]

But *The Singing Detective* is not just about the expiation of repressed guilt; it's Potter's most optimistic response so far to the world of multinationals and conglomerates that flourished in the 1980s. Jack Barker in *Sufficient Carbohydrate* was the first victim of that phenomenon, his family firm having been taken over by an American company which had started calling the shots. Philip Marlow is the second, for in a subplot Nicola, his former wife, is plotting to swindle Marlow out of the proceeds of a film script he has written which they have managed to sell to an American producer. Those to whom you are closest are the first to betray you: Marlow is exploited by his former wife, just as Jessica, the protagonist of *Blackeyes*, is abused by her uncle.

What distinguishes Marlow is the successful resolution of the process by which he pieces together the clues from his past. His recovery is a kind of miracle by which he both heals his body and restores the sense of his unique, sovereign self; as Potter remarks, 'It attempted to show accurately what it is like to be stripped of everything and then to attempt, via cheap fiction and a mix of memory – distorted memory, invented memory and real memory – to reassemble oneself. It was, in itself, a pilgrimage, an act of optimism that began with total nihilistic depair and ended with someone walking out into the world.'[67]

Blackeyes is another story of psychological detection, but with a very different outcome. Since the screenplay remains unpublished, my quotations come from Potter's 1987 novel on which it was based. It is layered in a manner similar to *The Singing Detective*, for one of its characters, Maurice James Kingsley, an aged man of letters, has written a successful novel called *Sugar Bush*, the plot of which is analysed in parallel with Potter's account of the last day of Kingsley's life; *Sugar Bush*

> told the story of a young model from her first audition to her final tragedy, a span of less than a decade. Later critics would come to see that the author had in truth made little attempt to give the unfortunate girl any sort of character or personality, but for the moment, at least, this sparseness was heralded as a fine example of an essential economy of art capable of bringing to life a touchingly enigmatic and elusive young woman.[68]

Potter is having fun at the reviewers' expense; not for the first time, they are wrong. Kingsley's failure to give personality to his heroine, Blackeyes, is evidence of both artistic incompetence and a contempt for women. What's worse, his narrative not only dwells on Blackeyes' passivity, but celebrates it: 'Her perfectly formed oval of a face was a blank upon which male desire could be projected. Her luminous, jet-like eyes said nothing, and so said everything. She was pliable. She was there to be invented, in any posture, any words, over and over again, in ejaculatory longing.'[69] Any reviewer who finds such a personality enigmatic and elusive is missing the point. The 'ejaculatory longing' with which male desire reinvents Blackeyes confirms the suspicion that she's little more than an animated pin-up, and that her suicidal drowning is the ultimate act of sexual repression. All of which can be traced back to Kingsley, whose theology has much in common with that of Jack Black and Mr Bates. When his niece Jessica asks him what is the point, he answers: 'Life, do you mean? Random molecules, dear girl. There is no point.'[70]

If Kingsley's materialism seems ironic in view of his tendency to recite Wordsworth and Tennyson,[71] that only goes to show how superficial is his literary expertise, along with his floppy bow-tie and 'Literary Voice', which 'suggested antique spellings and tadpole-sized commas even when there were none'.[72] If he is too vain and dishonest to admit that he has written anything less than another *Middlemarch*, the absence of humanity from his life and work is reflected in his unacknowledged exploitation of Jessica's life, from whose letters and experiences he takes the material for his novel. When they lunch together he eyes her 'fine figure', privately denies that she has any brains, and allows her to pay.[73] When she attempts to explain the psychological motivation behind her former promiscuity, he dismisses her with the thought that 'You let yourself be rogered by any Johnny who cared to ask.'[74]

The success of *Sugar Bush* leads Jessica to regard her uncle as the 'thief and plunderer' of her life,[75] and when he refers to it she cannot help but protest to herself 'My book, *my* book.'[76] Potter's novel *Blackeyes* also belongs to her for, despite appearances, she, rather than her uncle, is its protagonist. Kingsley's appropriation of her life is bad enough, but what she really resents are the darker crimes, memories of which it has revived. Looking down on the London mews where she lives, breathing the city air, 'bearing foulness at its heart',

> She had come to understand that women were so used to having their lives expressed in terms of male voices, male judgements, male desires, and the manipulative power of men, that they did not have the same hold on the substance of their beings as their oppressors had. But the loss and the confusion she was feeling at the partly opened window came from even deeper apprehensions of abuse.[77]

Potter's prose is no more relaxed than his dialogue; its power lies in the conviction of its rhetoric, and the way in which, as here, it informs the world in which his characters move. Few readers would mistake him for a feminist, but Jessica's ruminations attest to a greater intuition of powerlessness than his other works might lead us to suspect. More importantly, they take us almost to the core of Jessica's world. She has lost control of the very substance of her being, reworked by her uncle into the passive heroine he finally destroys. If he has not taken the same liberties with her body, her sensation of insubstantiality – intensified by the yearning for 'real solidities, real textures'[78] – suggests that he might as well have done.

The razor-sharp precision of Potter's phrasing, 'deeper apprehensions of abuse', carries its shock waves into the novel's conclusion. At first its significance is unclear; though, as we have seen, Kingsley does take a mercilessly utilitarian attitude to his niece, his requisitioning of her life-story stops short of physical abuse. But Jessica's apprehensions surface elsewhere. Lunching with Kingsley, she notices a 'fleck of veal . . . on his lip. Dead calf, she thought. The slaughter of babies':

> She looked like someone who had just seen an evil spirit. Whatever it was sucked the blood from her face, and scooped deep down into the tunnels of her eyes. And then the blanched surprise turned back on itself to become a formidable hatred.[79]

The materiality for which Jessica craves is served up, with interest, in this vividly intense reaction to Kingsley's minor impropriety. Slightly overwritten, vaguely reminiscent of Chandler or Hammett, the impassioned manner of the prose, with its associations of underworlds, criminality, and paranoid psychosis, extends the psychological drama without trivialising it. The fleck of veal on Kingsley's lip turns him for a moment into a child-murderer; the 'tunnels' of Jessica's eyes hint at subterranean forces; the evil spirit that sucks her blood may be a snake or a leech, but it is assuredly the spectre of some past event; and there is little doubt as to who inspires her final surge of hatred.

Vain and self-deceiving as ever, Kingsley 'twisted his head around to make sure that he was not the object of such venom'.[80] Even if her attentions were directed elsewhere, Jessica is not at this moment entirely balanced, not quite herself. She is as powerless in the grip of her own passion as is Blackeyes. However, this scene being set prior to the composition of *Sugar Bush*, Jessica's hostility is inspired, not by Kingsley's unacknowledged appropriation of her life-story, but by something previous to it.

Its cause is twice described. In Chapter Sixteen, halfway through Potter's novel, Kingsley recalls how when Jessica was a small girl he took her out for the day in London. They sailed a toy boat on the Serpentine and he bought her a doll which sang 'Clementine'. In the late evening he drove her home through the country, but on the way turned off the road and stopped the car. He was stricken suddenly by a feeling that something was wrong: 'What is it? said an older, deeper part of his head, at the same time. What dreadful thing is it that has happened?' The voice from 'an older, deeper part of his head' tips another wink in the direction of the psychological underworld into which the true drama has been submerged, but Kingsley prefers to interpret it as an acknowledgement of the mediocrity of his talent:

He saw that the novel he had so recently finished, his third, was banal and dishonest, even though it had been praised to low heavens by those who read it. Worse still, the book had been preceded by two others which were no less meretricious. Oh, woe: then woe: and then more woe. And each inner cry without a trace of irony, that normal compensation for the defeated, the disappointed and the self-deceiving.[81]

The cold comfort of 'low heavens' buries his literary aspirations for good, and, were we in any doubt, even the inner lament that accompanies this bolt of recognition is stripped of the saving grace of irony. This is no joke. Those last accusatory blows, 'the defeated, the disappointed and the self-deceiving', are the moral co-ordinates that pin him down. His recollecting mind is aware of the 'ache at the back of the sky, a tingle of nerves behind the shapes, a cry beyond the sounds',[82] but has repressed their cause.

Repression is as surely the theme of *Blackeyes* as it was of *The Singing Detective*; the difference is that *Blackeyes* traces a journey not of discovery but of damnation. For Potter, the act of recognition, of conscious acceptance, is redemptive; conversely, the forces that we repress, and that warp our behaviour, are the source of tragedy. In this sense, *Blackeyes* is a fully tragic work. Where Marlow was guided out of his hell by the psychotherapist Dr Gibbon, Jessica is trapped in hers with Kingsley. The abuse of which she is conscious is, as we have seen, his theft of her life-story. But she never consciously acknowledges the deeper apprehension that underlies her disproportionate sense of grievance and hatred for him, attributing it entirely to the success of *Sugar Bush*.

Its true origins are glimpsed in her nightmare in the novel's final pages, which retraces her day in London with Kingsley when she was a little girl, and includes a detail he omitted. On the way back, having stopped the car on a quiet track off the main road, Kingsley turned to her.

Sweet Jessie. Sweet, sweet Jessie. Sweet little, good little, pretty little baby. How well she remembered the words that he, presumably, thought she had forgotten. There was darkness at the windows, the new dolly was pressed tightly against her, and the far door was swinging open.

'Sweet Jessie,' he had said, leaning across on his knees, and kissing the top of her head. He had a snake with him which,

mysteriously became a sticky part of his body, and he made her
stroke it, pulling at her hand when she tried to stop. She both
knew and did not know what was happening. In the end, the
snake frothed at its single eye, or mouth, and she cried out in
alarm. He put his hand over her mouth and wept himself until
they were both silent. She could smell the tobacco on his fingers
and then the sweat on his body, and the arm or the leg of the doll
dug into her leg.[83]

Having robbed his niece of her innocence Kingsley buys himself an
insight he did not want; his abuse of her reveals to him the absence,
or failure, of the qualities that might have guaranteed his worth as
an artist. By his own account his work is 'meretricious' – showily or
falsely attractive – an epithet that applies also to his character.
Placing his hand over Jessica's mouth, Kingsley commits the
original repressive act of which the writing of *Sugar Bush* is a
repetition. His abuse of her itself prefigures the 'ejaculatory longing'
with which Jessica's image, and that of her fictional *alter ego*
Blackeyes, will be reproduced in later life.

But Jessica sees this only in sleep, so that its significance is not
fully vouchsafed: 'She both knew and did not know what was
happening.' Unlike those of Marlow, her wounds are never healed;
the snake-like spirit that sucked the blood out of her face in the
restaurant is never exorcised. All the same, the deep, undischarged
vein of suffering and resentment enables her finally to take revenge
on Kingsley and all the men who have abused her. One evening she
invites her Uncle to her flat for dinner, but he becomes drunk and
falls to the floor:

She stood above him for a while, contemplating him. He closed
his eyes in a twitchy flutter, but they would not stay shut, so he
sighed deeply, and found within himself his old literary boom.
    "'So sad,'" he said, "'so strange, the days that are no more.'"
    Jessica drove her foot into his ribs, but her expression stayed as
one in the calmness of contemplation, and did not distort.[84]

The 'old literary boom' is that self-regarding element in Kingsley's
character that blinds him to the truth and foils his writerly hopes.
On the other hand, although he probably does not know it, his
critical instincts are for once correct. The poem he drunkenly quotes
in this passage, and continues to recite as Jessica batters him to

death, serves as an unconscious recognition of the events he has edited out of his memory. But it is also a potent expression of remorse at the passing of the visionary power that made the earth sing with magic, and from which Potter continues to draw imaginative strength:

> Tears, idle tears, I know not what they mean,
> Tears from the depth of some divine despair
> Rise in the heart, and gather to the eyes,
> In looking on the happy autumn-fields,
> And thinking of the days that are no more.
>
> Fresh as the first beam glittering on a sail,
> That brings our friends up from the underworld,
> Sad as the last which reddens over one
> That sinks with all the love below the verge;
> So sad, so fresh, the days that are no more.
>
> Ah, sad and strange as in dark summer dawns
> The earliest pipe of half-awakened birds
> To dying ears, when unto dying eyes
> The casement slowly grows a glimmering square;
> So sad, so strange, the days that are no more.
>
> Dear as remembered kisses after death,
> And sweet as those by hopeless fancy feigned
> On lips that are for others; deep as love,
> Deep as first love, and wild with all regret;
> O Death in Life, the days that are no more!

Potter's most recent work for television, *Lipstick on Your Collar* (1993), emerges from the blackness that pervaded *Blackeyes*, into comedy. It needs to be said that the production of *Lipstick* turned out to be the least successful of a Potter work to date, partly because the comic element was too strained and deliberate to induce laughter. In fact, comedy has never been Potter's strength. Humour in his writing tends towards the sardonic rather than the light-hearted, and despite some fine acting the production never quite found its correct pitch.

Lipstick reworks themes familiar from *Pennies From Heaven*. Francis Francis, its clumsy protagonist, is similar to Arthur Parker in that he is a romantic; to him, Pushkin and Chekhov 'are saying the world is other than it is, or simpler than it is, or are bemoaning lost love'.[85] The problem with romanticism for Potter's characters, however, is that it can be delusive. Uncle Kingsley spouted Wordsworth and Tennyson only as a means of covering up the unfathomable hell within; Bernard in *Cream in my Coffee* was misled by youthful impetuousness into proposing marriage to a woman he could not really love; and, most tellingly of all, a too-fervent belief in the ideal world described by popular music prevented Arthur Parker from controlling his life: 'He could never assemble himself, he wasn't capable of that, and although there was a certain shape to his life it was one that he could never get hold of; the songs prevented him getting a hold of it.'[86] As in *Blackeyes*, the seeds of tragedy lie in self-deception, in the failure to acknowledge one's unique, sovereign self.

Being a comedy, *Lipstick* needs to project Francis' development beyond his unquestioning attachment to the world described by Pushkin. This is foreshadowed in the first scene in which he appears, when his expertise in Russian is put to the test by Major Church:

FRANCIS:
> *Pyeryedo mnoy yavilas ty*
> *Kak mimolyotnoye vidyenye . . .*

CHURCH: What?
FRANCIS: (*Uneasily*)
> 'You stood before me
> Like a momentary vision –'

CHURCH: Did I?
But Francis has an awkward young man's suddenly flushed imagination.
FRANCIS: Sir. He is remembering the very first time he –
CHURCH: Had a bunk-up.
FRANCIS: No, sir!
CHURCH: No?
FRANCIS: (*Twitches*) No, sir. The first time he met this – this enchantingly lovely young lady Anna, sir. And how now that he has seen her again, his heart is – is – (*Falters under the stare*) Sorry, sir.
CHURCH: (*With precision*) Tosh.[87]

That final direction to the actor playing Church, 'With precision', is more significant than may at first appear. It confronts Francis with a lesson he has to learn if he is to survive – that the romanticism of nineteenth-century Russian literature is misleading because it excludes from its vision lust and carnality. Potter confronts the music of Pushkin's verse, with its unquenchable yearnings for the ideal woman, with the physical facts of human life. In fact, the humiliating lesson doled out to Francis in his first scene provides the running joke of *Lipstick*; throughout, he is faced with a physical reality he would rather ignore. At the end of Episode Five, for instance, he visits the widowed Sylvia to console her, but, as she breaks down, he 'is moved, and forgets all that he had meant to say. . . . Her breast is exposed, quivering with her sobs. He looks at it. He cannot help it. His hands reach – '.[88] As he later admits to his Aunt Vickie, 'I didn't realise how much of the animal is in me. . . . A beast, I am.'[89] Even more strikingly, in Episode Two, Francis' confession of his affection for Sylvia is overheard by her husband, Corporal Berry. In retaliation, Berry drags him to the lavatory cubicle in which he has just defecated, and holds him over the unflushed pan:

> BERRY: Go on! Look at it! Look at it!
> FRANCIS: No – ach – no – o –
> BERRY: Go on! Take a closer look! Shit to shit!
> Sound of Francis starting to heave. And then – mercifully – the creak of the ancient chain, and the sound of the lavatory flushing.[90]

Berry unwittingly gives Francis an important psychological lesson, for Francis consistently refuses to recognise the animal part of himself (and others). And just in case we are in any doubt, Potter makes excrement the motif of this episode.

Hopper and Francis are employed to translate Russian documents in the War Office during the Cold War in 1956, but, as Hopper explains, owing to a shortage of the real thing, the Russians have used many of the documents on which they are working as toilet paper: 'Our bloke creeps up behind the bucket when a bloody bolshevik has a shite (*Looks at BERRY*) A corporal, I should think. And he grabs the paper. Hot from the press. . . . What difference does one more little bit of shit make? The whole bloody job stinks anyway.'[91]

As this speech indicates, Hopper has no illusions. He is, in fact, Francis' undeluded counterpart, and, as such, his role in the drama is partly choric. Which underlines a crucial distinction between *Pennies From Heaven* and *Lipstick*. All of the musical interludes originate in Hopper's mind, and exist not to project an unattainable ideal, like those imagined by Arthur Parker (or like those that might be expected from Francis), but to comment, often satirically, on the drama. Potter first uses music in this way in the 'Dry Bones' routine in *The Singing Detective*;[92] it is fully exploited, however, in *Lipstick*.

Take, for instance, Hopper's daydream accompanying the Stargazers' 'I See the Moon', which is like some scatological cartoon combining the Suez crisis with life in the War Office:

> Bernwood's lunacy is now choreographed, with music, into a crazed 'Arabian' fantasy, with belly dancers, Ali Baba pots, a pantomime camel and hundreds of party balloons. At the windows, Hopper's fantasized 'dream girl' floats past on a magic carpet. 'Arab brigands' threaten with scimitars, some of the yashmak belly dancers turn out to be hideous, or male, and the camel defecates amply enough to provide Hopper, Francis and Berry with ammunition to sling at the officers. Hopper remains the orchestrator, the impresario, gleefully beating out the lyrics with lunatic abandon, happily turning his superiors into wobble-faced loons.[93]

The fantasy suggests that Hopper is clearer-sighted about political matters than he may appear. One of the subjects of *Lipstick* is the crisis in Britain – not arising merely from Suez, but from its divestiture of an imperial past. Bernwood's lunacy arises from his inability to accept his country's subsidiary role in world affairs. As he remarks at one point, 'Something has happened to us. As a people, I mean. And I never thought I'd live to see the day. Or, rather, the night. The long, long night. The darkness and the shame and then – '.[94] In Hopper's dream, the Officers represent the forces of conservativism, those who, like Bernwood, wish to send troops to Suez in order to 'Hit them hard! Hard! Fucking Hard!'[95] The lower ranks, on the other hand – Hopper, Francis, and Berry – are more pragmatic. Not only do they accept Britain's inability to put down the Arabs, but they collude with them: Hopper's dream-girl is Egyptian, and a conveniently prolific camel helps them fight their superiors. This symbolic mock-battle foreshadows the declassification of British society during the 1960s. In fact, we might correctly infer from Hopper's fantasy that one reason for the collapse of the class system was Britain's decline as a world power during the 1950s – a decline in which the Suez crisis was instrumental.[96]

Hopper's daydream seems mad, but is nevertheless politically acute. True insanity is a product of self-deception: Bernwood descends into a crazed melancholy brought on by his outdated vision of Britain's imperial past; Francis' Uncle Fred flies into a rage at the Americanisation of Robin Hood as portrayed on the wireless; and Francis himself is in danger of driving himself crazy by idealising Sylvia. Like Bernard in *Cream in my Coffee*, he is too intoxicated with romantic notions to see that he is in love, not with her, but with a fiction borrowed from literature.

But he is not completely blind. Just before the incident that leads to her husband's death, he witnesses her assault of Harold Atterbow, the cinema organist from whom she has been receiving money for sex, and reflects 'that perhaps, after all, she is not the ideal love from Pushkin or any of the Romantic poets'.[97]

As I have suggested, Hopper's daydream indicates that Britain's future lies in accepting the rise of America as the main cultural and political force in the world; it is not surprising, then, that Francis is redeemed by an American – Colonel Trekker's daughter, Lisa. She shares his love of Russian literature, and is a more appropriate foil for the delusions arising from it.

It would be tempting to suggest that the moral journey undertaken by Potter's protagonists tends to echo the motif of Aeneas' underworld journey in *Aeneid* Book VI. Aeneas descends into the underworld to meet his dead father, Anchises, who shows him the past and the future. The powerful images in *Lipstick* of Francis being held over an unflushed lavatory and, later, of him tumbling into Corporal Berry's unfilled grave, suggest that he is Aeneas' comic counterpart. This comparison is supported by Aunt Vickie's remark in Episode One that the Put-U-Up on which Francis will be sleeping was where '*you* might have been first thought of'.[98] That brazen reference to the primal scene hints that he might undergo a psychological journey similar to that made by Philip Marlow, whose personality has indeed been warped by the repressed memory of his mother having sex. But this is not to be.

One reason why *Lipstick* is less dramatically satisfying than Potter's earlier work is that, unlike Aeneas, Arthur Parker or Philip Marlow, Francis remains unchanged at its conclusion. He is as much the slave of romantic notions derived from books at the end as he was at the start. His thwarted love for Sylvia, and witnessing of

Corporal Berry's gruesome death, grant him no deeper understanding of himself or the world around him. At the end of Episode
One, Francis is characterised by 'yearning and hunger',[99] but he
never develops beyond that. Hopper has a more engaging inner life;
it is, after all, from him that the musical interludes originate – set
pieces that combine worldliness with imagination. He is, finally,
paired up with Sylvia, but his acceptance of her moral failings –
which Potter goes to some pains to emphasise in order to explain
her unsuitability for Francis – is glossed over. Nor, for that matter, is
Francis' pairing with Lisa, the daughter of an oil baron, anything
more than convenient. Fairy-tale endings need to be earned by the
characters if they are not to betray the plot into superficiality. This is
the biggest cop-out of all: Potter finally surrenders his characters to
a glib romanticism that he elsewhere regards more critically.

The narrative flaws in *Lipstick* are only underlined by the care and
lavishness of the finished production. They are all the more
surprising in view of the fact that Potter has not previously failed
to compel our attention through his protagonists; if anything, he has
been criticised for over-investing them with pain and passion.

Only in the final stages of writing have I heard that Potter will be
dead by the time this book gets into print. I selected him as one of
my subjects because of his contemporaneity – a quality I do not
hesitate to affirm. If he has chosen to work in a medium
characterised by its disposability, I believe that his plays will
continue to speak with the immediacy and urgency generated at the
time of their first viewing, whether in print or through repeat
showings on television. His contemporaneity is poignantly felt as I
write, not just because, as I have observed, he grapples with the
same issues that concerned the Psalmist, Wordsworth, Coleridge,
Tennyson, and the other great poets of our literature, but because he
continues, in his last months, to compose dramas he will not live to
see performed. *Karaoke* and *Cold Lazarus* will probably be
transmitted posthumously on both BBC and Channel Four. A hint
of the central theme of *Karaoke* may be found in *Potter on Potter*, in a
moving statement that takes us to the heart of his work. Discussing
his use of popular songs in *Pennies From Heaven*, he observes:

> They are both ludicrous and banal, reducing everything to the
> utmost simplification, but also, at the same time, saying, 'Yes,
> there is another way of seeing, there is another way, there is
> another reality.' It is this that makes karaoke, in an odd sense,

popular too. It offers instant gratification, and instant stardom for a few minutes, but it's also about the world being other than it is. Singing is in a line of descent from the psalms, a way of puncturing reality, the ordered structure of things as they are. As soon as we start to sing, dance, remember, things are *not* as they are. We are no longer just gathering in the hay, as it were. It's a weird thing to do – a non-animal thing to do. The angel in us.[100]

4

Simon Gray: Numbness of the Heart

It was evening, you see, and I was – well, in that corner, over there, where the hollyhocks are, doing a spot of weeding. I stood up, rather too quickly, I suppose, momentarily a touch dizzy – a touch *something* – or touched *by* something – and the house, the garden – well, you remember that first afternoon when we all met, and Nigel and Natalie were here hiding all the time, but you were so frightened and thought they'd been trampled to death by old Tomalin's cattle – and when we came back, all of us absolutely distraught, convinced they were dead – we suddenly heard them, their voices, they were laughing, and so was Ben – and you and Harry. I don't think I've ever seen such joy on human faces. Well, that evening I heard it all again. Seemed to hear it all again, and I thought, yes, I thought, there is a spirit. A human spirit, a divine spirit even, they meet sometimes, by accident, if you're lucky. Or a touch dizzy. In an English garden.[1]

This speech by Ronnie, the clergyman in Simon Gray's most recent work, *Hidden Laughter* (1990), reveals a deeply felt aspiration, mediated through layers of shared cultural memories that renew, rather than merely exploit, the language. The recognition of a 'human spirit, a divine spirit even' invokes, for instance, the strange command at the conclusion of Wordsworth's *Nutting*:

> Then, dearest Maiden! move along these shades
> In gentleness of heart; with gentle hand
> Touch, – for there is a Spirit in the woods. (lines 54–6)

Intimations of this kind carry an awesome power, reminding us that poetry can still connect with the substance of the world, for what counts most is not their ecological significance, but the intensity with which they assert 'gentleness of heart'. The ethical implications are recognised in *Hidden Laughter*, where the spirit is emphatically human, possibly divine. Standing in the garden, Ronnie seems to hear the laughter of children, and recalls 'such joy on human faces'.

Although we see the events that lead up to this epiphany, its climax is not acted out before us, nor could it be. It is an internal drama admitting us to a world of glorious possibility in which we are delivered from our worst fears and find ourselves at one with our surroundings; the garden is transformed into something greater than the sum of its parts, partaking of those within it, and of something beyond. If only for a moment, its potential as a 'little acre of paradise'[2] is realised. The same process is at work in the lines from Eliot's *Burnt Norton* which provide the more obvious source for Ronnie's speech:

> Go, said the bird, for the leaves were full of children,
> Hidden excitedly, containing laughter.
> Go, go, go, said the bird: human kind
> Cannot bear very much reality.
> Time past and time future
> What might have been and what has been
> Point to one end, which is always present.[3]

The generation of a meditative, monitory tone, a verbal gravity that roots the verse in the immediate concerns of our lives, is what 'maturity' means to Eliot. For, like Wordsworth, he is concerned less with ecology than with ethics. Although the higher reality of a paradisal vision cannot be sustained, it may nevertheless inform our conduct in the fallen world. Only by reclaiming innocence through insight can we find the still point of the turning world.

The process of recovery is no abstraction; without it, there is nothing to regulate our conduct towards others, or even our sanity. When Gray's protagonists blind themselves to the voice of admonition that speaks to them from the past, they invariably lose themselves. The eponymous Butley in Gray's 1970 play is a case in point. Ben Butley lectures in English at the University of London but, as is common among academics, he's lost touch with the world. No-one phones him, he can't remember his own daughter's name, and has fallen into the trap of living vicariously through his male students. In one scene Miss Heasman, one of his undergraduates, reads him an essay on *A Winter's Tale*:

MISS HEASMAN: 'The central image is drawn from nature, to counterpoint the imagery of the first half of the play, with its stress on sickness and deformity. Paradoxically, *A Winter's Tale* of a frozen soul –'

BEN: Bit fish-mongery, that.

MISS HEASMAN: '- is therefore thematically and symbolically about revitalization.'

BEN: Sorry. Re-whatalization?

MISS HEASMAN: Re-*vit*alization.[4]

Butley mistakenly believes the joke to be on Miss Heasman but it is he who is estranged from his infant child; like Leontes, he is spiritually dead. A moment later he asks Miss Heasman whether she can see and aims the desk light at her essay, but forgets to switch it on. Illumination is never granted to Butley, a point made by the play's final action in which he returns to the anglepoise and finds that it is broken.

Simon Hench in *Otherwise Engaged* (1975) is similarly benighted. When he resists the advances of Davina, the girlfriend of his best friend, Jeff, it seems that his moral credentials are impeccable. After she has left he is visited at home by Wood, an old schoolfriend concerned about his young girlfriend, Joanna, whom he claims at first as his daughter. She has failed to return home after visiting Simon's office the evening before in the hope of finding employment as a designer of book covers.

SIMON: I can quite understand your worry –

WOOD: Can you? No, I don't think you can.

SIMON: No, perhaps not. But I don't really see how I can help you any further.

WOOD: Did you have it off with her?

SIMON: What? *What*?

WOOD: Did you have it off with her?

SIMON: Look, Wood, whatever your anxiety about your daughter, I really don't think, old chap, that you should insinuate yourself into people's homes and put a question like that to them. I mean, good God, you can't possibly expect me to dignify it with an answer, can you?

WOOD: In other words, you did.

SIMON: (*after a long pause*). In other words, I'm afraid I did. Yes. Sorry, old chap.[5]

Simon admits that he feels no shame, guilt or embarrassment because his involvement with Joanna was characteristically opportunistic and superficial. He is the opposite of Wood, who confesses to feeling 'incapacitated by devotion'. 'But you live together?' Simon asks.

> WOOD: She allows me to share the flat I've leased for her. We have different rooms – I sometimes sit on the side of her bed when she's in it. More often when she's not.
> SIMON: You're obviously in the grip of a passion almost Dante-esque in the purity of its hopelessness. You know, I really feel quite envious – for you every moment has its significance, however tortured. I just have to get by on my small pleasures and easy accommodations, my daily contentments . . .[6]

Simon's response, with its inadvertent cruelty and fraternal condescension, shows just how contemptuous he is of other people. The implied mockery in his invocation of Dante is deliberate, but whether he is fully aware of the smug confidence of such phrases as 'small pleasures and easy accommodations', or of the pain they must cause Wood, is questionable. Not that the point is either Simon's language or what it describes; it is, rather, his implied disregard for others' feelings, even those of his wife, Beth. For the last ten months she has been having an affair with Ned, one of her colleagues. Although he does not appear in the play, Ned is instantly recognisable as one of those blessed with clarity of vision, a character-type that recurs throughout Gray's work. His judgement of Simon is reported by Beth: 'He says you're one of those men who only give permission to little bits of life to get through to you. He says that while we may envy you your serenity, we should be revolted by the rot from which it stems. Your sanity is of the kind that causes people to go quietly mad around you.'[7] Serenity and sanity are merely a recasting of the 'small pleasures and easy accommodations' to which Simon confesses earlier, and in this context they carry the same hint of selfish complacency.

Ned's assessment of Simon is borne out by the play's structure, its central conceit being that he wishes to listen to a new recording of *Parsifal* but is prevented from doing so by a stream of uninvited visitors, Davina, Wood, Beth, and his brother, to whose anguish over a job application Simon remains oblivious. *Parsifal* concerns the need for spiritual regeneration but, just as Butley fails to learn from *A Winter's Tale*, Simon remains deaf to what Wagner's opera might tell him; he is otherwise engaged.

With a number of successful plays behind him, all dealing with contemporary situations, Gray turned, in *The Rear Column* (1978), to the five Victorian gentlemen left by Stanley for over a year on the banks of the Arruwimi river in the Congo in 1887. The medical orderly, Bonny, becomes a laudanum addict; Ward becomes emotionally deadened; Troup becomes a hypochondriac; Jameson colludes with the natives in the cannibalising of a young girl; and the commanding officer, Barttelot, becomes a sadistic murderer. 'One can't plan motives', Stanley remarks at the end of the play, 'only results', the implication being that he knew all along what would happen. This is underlined by Gray who observes that the central point of the play 'is not an assertion that the five Victorians behaved badly, but an implicit question about whether you or I or he could have behaved better'.[8]

The decline into barbarism does not take place overnight, and in fact Gray's characters make repeated attempts to stave it off. Ward invokes 'ratiocination', and Troup calls for 'a reasoned and proper discussion'. When this fails, they get drunk together on Christmas Eve and Troup declares that 'we've forged a bond – between us – that – that – speaking for myself I know will last to the end of my life.'[9] This may be sentimental, but the insight vouchsafed by Troup is not worthless. He recognises the importance of the 'human spirit' that so impresses Ronnie in *Hidden Laughter*, and which Gray sees as crucial in the regulation of human behaviour. Those without it, such as Ben Butley and Simon Hench, may survive, but they will do so in a state of perpetual lovelessness. In this light it is significant that the only member of Stanley's rear column to emerge with reputation intact is Bonny, the laudanum addict who allowed the thefts of opium to be blamed, significantly, on the most sentimental, and therefore the weakest of their number, Troup.

The staff of the Cambridge language school which provides the setting for *Quartermaine's Terms* (1981) are strangely similar to the officers and gentlemen of *The Rear Column*. They put up with their colleagues only for minutes at a time, and even then appear cruelly insensitive to each other. The only character to explain this is another of those who do not appear on stage – Susan, the daughter of one of the teachers, Henry Windscape. While doing her O-levels she has developed, her father reports,

quite an interest in – in – well, philosophical speculation, I
suppose it is, really – the other evening – she suddenly insisted –
in the middle of supper – she'd been very quiet until then – she
suddenly insisted that we couldn't prove that other people existed
– and that perhaps when we thought about them or remembered
them or saw and heard them even – we were actually just making
them up – and of course I took her up on this and attempted to
explain how it is we do know that other people exist including
people we don't know exist, if you follow – (*Laughing*.) and she
kept saying 'But you can't prove it, Daddy, you can't actually
prove it!' And she was right. I found myself getting quite tangled
in my own arguments.[10]

Henry is confounded because, although he likes to think of himself
as sympathetic to others, he and his colleagues tend to be as
solipsistic and self-serving as his daughter suggests. Distinct
realities besides his own do exist, but neither he nor any other
character in the play submits themselves to the awful daring of a
moment's surrender that would enable anyone else to share their
lives.[11] As if to emphasise this, Melanie, to whom Henry is at this
moment speaking, tells him how depressed she feels by the hatred
of her invalid mother and laments: 'What a fool I was not to – not to
marry you when you gave me the chance.'[12] Henry's response is
characteristic: 'There there, my dear, there there – mustn't think of
the past – it's the – the future – the future – there there –'.[13] The
phone rings, and he uses it as the excuse for a quick exit.

Susan's philosophical speculations determine the underlying
moral question of the play: in what sense do (or can) other people
exist for us? This is unintentionally adverted to first by Henry,
without prompting from his daughter, when he notes

this English thing about names, how we forget them the second
we hear them. . . . Unlike Americans for instance. I suppose
because we – the English that is – are so busy looking at the
person the name represents – or *not* looking, being English (*He
laughs*.) that we don't take in the name itself – whereas the
Americans, you see, make a point of beginning with the name –
when one's introduced they repeat it endlessly. 'This is Dennis
Meadle. Dennis Meadle, why hello Dennis, and how long have
you have been in this country Dennis, this is Dennis Meadle dear,

Dennis was just telling me how much he liked our fair city, weren't you Dennis . . .'[14]

Since Meadle's first name is actually Derek, Henry's point about the failure either to listen to people's names or to look at the person they represent is more or less self-proving. The joke in his view is on the Americans, but at least they observe the basic courtesy of remembering names. He continues his argument by suggesting that the English are 'more empirical' than the Americans, and 'don't learn your name until you yourself have taken on a complicated reality – you and your name grow, so to speak, in associated stages in our memories, until what you are as Dennis Meadle and the sounds Dennis Meadle are inseparable'.[15] If this process is susceptible to scientific proof, as Susan claims, it fails to distinguish human relationships from those involving dogs, cats, or inanimate objects. Henry has reduced the 'complicated reality' of other people to nothing more than the sum total of our recollected dealings with them, tacitly denying those metaphysical relations not anchored in time and place. He has initiated a discussion he is unable to finish, but the play as a whole takes his argument to its logical conclusion.

What reality can others have in the demented mind of St John Quartermaine, who has virtually no short-term memory, and is in any case too disregarding to register their feelings? In the opening scene his colleague, Mark Sackling, enters unshaven and looking ghastly (according to the stage directions). When Quartermaine questions him about his wife and son Mark bursts into tears, leading Quartermaine to ask, 'Something you had for breakfast, is it?' When Mark explains that his wife has left him, taking his son with her, Quartermaine merely corrects a misreading of her farewell note. 'You know, St. John,' Mark later says, 'you have an amazing ability not to let the world impinge on you.'[16] The full horror of this is realised at the beginning of Act Two when, in the staffroom, Henry asks Quartermaine what he did for half-term: 'Did you go away?'

QUARTERMAINE: Well, I – I no, I stayed here.
WINDSCAPE: Here!
QUARTERMAINE: Yes.
WINDSCAPE: Oh, in Cambridge, you mean? Just for a moment I thought you meant actually *here* – in this room – I think, perhaps because the last time I saw you, you were sitting in exactly the same place in very much that position – as if you haven't moved all week.[17]

Just for a moment, before deceiving himself, Henry has glimpsed
the horrifying truth: Quartermaine's terms are fuller than those of
his colleagues. So uninvolved in others' lives is he that he has
nothing better to do than spend the half term in his armchair in the
staffroom. Quartermaine exemplifies the philosophical hell pro-
posed by Susan, in which we 'couldn't prove that other people
existed – and that perhaps when we thought about them or
remembered them or saw and heard them even – we were actually
just making them up'.

If this serves as a compelling explanation for the behaviour of
Quartermaine and his colleagues, it will not do as a philosophy of
life – not unless we nurture totalitarian tendencies, that is. Torture,
mass murder, genocide; all these things are justifiable if we deprive
other people of their objective reality and regard them as figments of
our imagination. Quartermaine's supreme indifference to those
around him is the most benign possible manifestation of this. But
the play's critique of Susan's reductive philosophy does not end
here. She fails to account, of course, for love, the reality of which is
affirmed in Melanie's unrequited devotion for Henry. Nor can it
account for those peculiar moments, uninvited, unpremeditated,
unintellected, when our conscious mind is granted some transforming insight, and when we feel that we are greater than we know. The
chief exponent of such experience is, ironically, Quartermaine.
Though in the normal course of events he appears incapable of
engaging with the outside world, and speaks little if at all to those
around him, he is suddenly brought to life by a chance remark by
Melanie about swans, which leads him to recall how,

> oh, just the other day, you know – on the Cam – drifting behind a
> punt – and they were all shouting and drinking champagne and –
> and it was just drifting behind them – so calm – and I remember
> there used to be oh! a dozen or so – they came every year to a
> pond near my aunt's – when I was – was and I could hear their
> wings – great wings beating – in the evenings when I was lying in
> bed – it could be quite – quite frightening even after I knew what
> was making the noise – and then the next morning there they'd be
> – a dozen of them or so – drifting – drifting around – and it was
> hard to imagine – their long necks twining and their way of
> drifting – all that – that power – those wings beating – I wonder
> where they went to.[18]

Quartermaine's grammatical incoherence should not deceive us into thinking, as does Melanie, who politely tells him to either shut up or go away, that these are the ramblings of a mind in tatters. On the contrary, the lucidity of this interval is underlined by the emotional intensity at the heart of his recollection: 'it could be quite – quite frightening even after I knew what was making the noise'. Reason fails to assuage the young boy's apprehension because the sound of the swans has a power transcending its physical reality; just as the perceptions of all children are, on occasion, imaginatively enhanced, so those of the young Quartermaine are impervious to logical explanation. Even in adulthood, though dead to the concerns of those around him, he remains irrevocably altered by that early experience.

This lingering remnant of humanity in Quartermaine's decayed psyche saves the play from tragedy, for those unnaturally potent early recollections provide the strongest possible argument against the idea that the perceived world is a mental construct. His recollection of the swans' strangely heightened power suggests that, however detached he appears, he remains in touch, at some deep level, with human emotion. This is confirmed by the echo of Yeats' *The Wild Swans at Coole*, where swans are an image of enduring vitality:

> Their hearts have not grown old;
> Passion or conquest, wander where they will,
> Attend upon them still. (lines 22–4)

It is symptomatic of the play's underlying optimism that Yeats' worst fear, that he will one day awaken 'To find they have flown away' (line 30), is not realised by Quartermaine, whose memory of the swans persists, along with the emotion attached to them.

Henry offers further cause for hope. Though unable to disprove his daughter's bleak view of the world through rational argument, his instinctive feeling that it is incorrect is confirmed by a subsequent experience on his caravanning expedition during the summer holidays:

It really was most – extraordinary – one morning at about six it was, I was trying to plug the leak – it was right over little Fanny's bunk – and so she was awake and so was Ben – and Susan hadn't slept at all – so it was all rather – rather fraught, with tempers fraying – but Fanny she'd gone outside to the loo, as a matter of fact – and suddenly she called us – all of us – told us to put on our wellies and macs and come out and look – and we did – and there – silhouetted against the sky was the most – the most –[19]

We never learn what was so extraordinary, silhouetted against the sky, because Henry is interrupted. He later tells Mark that it was sufficiently remarkable to inspire Fanny to write 'a small sort of prose poem about it'[20] – indicating that whether or not Henry himself understands his experience on anything deeper than a purely aesthetic level, it has much in common with Quartermaine's swans.

In both cases the vision remains in the memory to revitalise the mind, providing what Wordsworth called 'A fructifying virtue'.[21] But if the play stops short of tragedy it nevertheless presents a world in which Quartermaine must finally be betrayed by the likes of Henry – just as, in *King Lear*, Shakespeare confronts Lear's eventual belief that his relationship with Cordelia is immortal ('we'll wear out,/ In a wall'd prison, packs and sets of great ones,/ That ebb and flow by th' moon')[22] with a reality in which the likes of Edmund can sign death-warrants. If Gray is willing to entertain romantic notions, he refuses to let us believe that they can alter human nature.

This is not quite tragedy, but it amounts very nearly to a tragic view of life. As Madame Pernelle remarks in Gray's exemplary adaptation of *Tartuffe*, 'When you were a child, my child, I told you again and again that virtue is for ever persecuted in this world, that though the wicked die, wickedness itself lives on, flourishing always.'[23]

By the same token, the emotional impact of *The Common Pursuit* (1986) arises less from our knowledge of its characters' sexual infidelities, deceptions and cruelties, than from their casual betrayal of the ideals they shared as Cambridge undergraduates. Having shown them destroying each others' lives, Gray returns us in the final scene of the play to Stuart's rooms in College 20 years ago, where he is addressing his friends on the new literary magazine they are planning, and reporting the advice given him by a noted poet, Hubert Stout:

What we need to talk about now isn't simply what we want for our first few issues but our whole future. One very important thing Hubert Stout said is that, above all, we've got to be very

careful. Take into account all the things that could go wrong, all
the traps that other people have fallen into when starting out on
something like this. That's the only way we'll survive. By
knowing what it is we are about to give the world, precisely.[24]

As the innocent messenger of what the audience may be inclined to
read less as friendly advice than as a prophecy of failure, Stuart
stands to lose most by this speech – and, indeed, by this point the
audience is aware that Marigold, his future wife of over 15 years,
will spend most of that time having an affair with his best friend,
Martin, and finally divorce him, marry Martin and have his child.
As in the plays of Dennis Potter, the first to betray us, sexually or
otherwise, are inevitably those we most trust.[25] All of which makes
it doubly painful that immediately after Stuart has spoken Marigold
says, 'Absolutely'; 'Yes', Martin repeats, 'Absolutely.'

But these ruthlessly impacted ironies serve not merely to expose
naïveté on Stuart's part and bad faith on Marigold's; Gray has
quietly, deftly, pulled off a remarkable *coup de théâtre*, focusing the
play's full emotional weight on a single speech (much as Bennett
does at the end of *Me, I'm Afraid of Virginia Woolf*). It is poignant
enough that Stout's warnings should have extended beyond the
magazine to the moral fabric of their lives, for he must have realised
the futility of such admonitions. Because the lessons of life cannot be
learned in any way other than through experience, it is doubly
moving that Stuart so readily accepts the assumption that 'all the
things that could go wrong' may be guarded against. Unlike Nick,
who gets on in the world by lying, or Peter, who finds his affairs
more compelling than his marriage, Stuart never forsakes the ideals
invested in his magazine. Perhaps more than any other implication
of those telescoped, compounded ironies, this unlocks the play's
emotional reserves; for if it makes Stuart a fool, how can it help also
but lend him a certain heroic aspect, as invariably happens when
noble beliefs meet with failure? How can it help, come to that, but
reflect well on all the characters, none of whom sets out in bad faith?
If nothing else, the play affirms that it is better to have believed,
however vainly, than never to have believed at all. The insane
sexual jealousy suffered by Mark Melon in *The Holy Terror* (staged
originally as *Melon* in 1987) derives from precisely that moral
vacuum. Confessing his sins in a lecture to a women's institute he
declares: 'You see, ladies, please believe me, you must believe me,
please, when I say . . . (*Stares towards them*) that I still don't know

what the truth is. No, I don't.' As one who 'had the meaning but missed the experience',[26] Melon is more alienated than any of the characters in *The Common Pursuit*, since they at least can draw strength from Stuart's declaration of intent.

The most powerful affirmation of this comes not from Stuart but from Humphry. As the clearest-sighted of them Humphry is the conscience of the play; it is he who, significantly, studies moral sciences as an undergraduate, a subject that in one way or another remains his speciality. In later years, when he has become a Cambridge don, Martin tries to get him to write a book on Wagner but he fails to complete it. 'You mustn't give it up', says Martin, 'You mustn't.'

> HUMPHRY: Yes, I must. I've got the scholarship, and the judgement, but not the imagination. Everything I've written about him reduces him to my own sort of size. Which makes him too small to be interesting to me. You see I've discovered I have a slight flaw after all. Moral, I think, rather than intellectual. I diminish what I most admire.
> MARTIN: But – well, mightn't it help if you published *something*? What about a monograph? If not on Wagner, somebody else. What about our publishing your fellowship dissertation?
> HUMPHRY: It's on Hegel, Martin. In German, mostly. I stopped believing in it before I began it. I went through with it because it would allow me to work on the things I loved. Which I want to go on loving. Which is why I won't allow my intelligence to fix on them, ever again. I don't think I can be simpler, even for you.[27]

If Humphry's flaw is widely shared by academics, especially those working on literary matters, it is also, as he says, moral rather than intellectual. And as such it is a variation on the more widespread tendency at work throughout the play by which the things each character loves are betrayed or in some way compromised. Humphry's confession thus assumes a chilling significance when he exits for the last time, saying, 'I've got to be on my way if I'm going to just miss my train, and enjoy an hour and a half hanging around the station lavatory.'[28] Mankind cannot bear too much reality, and the burden of comprehending that of human behaviour – especially our own – is too much for most of us. That burden becomes plain when we learn that Humphry has been beaten to death by one of his pick-ups. As Martin says, 'We'd heard what he was getting up to. The risks he was taking. We all tried to warn him, but it was almost as if he *wanted* to be murdered.'[29] In this light Humphry's echo of Wilde has a grim appropriateness: 'Each man kills the thing he loves.'

Wilde's suggestion that the destructive urge is built-in, as ineluctable as the ageing process itself, is picked up in *The Holy Terror*. At the height of his sickness Melon meets Jacob, a gay friend, and asks after his sex life. 'Young Donald still giving you decent service?'

JACOB: David. He works at the box office at the National Theatre. As a matter of fact we've just split up.
MELON: Why?
JACOB: Oh, the usual reason, I expect. Because he didn't love me.
MELON: Oh, I shouldn't worry about it. Lots more where he comes from. And once you've cleaned out the box office you can run through the ushers. And then there's backstage . . .[30]

When Jacob, who is a doctor, tells him that he is sick, Melon retorts that 'You've forgotten what it's like to encounter a sane, robustly healthy, cheerful, fun-loving prankster of an Englishman.' Melon's self-diagnosis plays up the comedy, which seems to have been at Jacob's expense. But Jacob's assessment is correct, and what shocks most about their exchange is the interior paralysis, the numbness of the heart betrayed by Melon's assumption that Jacob's relationships are purely sexual. If Jacob's sad admission that David left 'Because he didn't love me' suggests otherwise, Melon misunderstands because he doesn't know what love is. It is no accident that the main symptom of his illness is his compulsive marital infidelity.

In one scene he is interviewing Gladys Powers, one of the authors he publishes, and puts his hand on her thigh. 'What are you doing?' she asks.

MELON: Groping you, of course. To find out whether you're still wearing stockings, or whether you've gone over to the other side. You have. Tights. Oh, Gladys!
GLADYS: Will you bloody well stop that?
MELON: Sorry, love. You usen't to mind –
GLADYS: Are you drunk? Or on pills or something?[31]

Melon's betrayals lead to a derangement that takes the form of an obsessive sexual jealousy of his wife's imagined affairs. But as his closing remarks emphasise, the circumstances of his case do not make his sickness unique: 'It could have happened to anyone. I insist upon that. Anyone. To you. Or to your husband. Or son. Or daughter. Or brother. To any of us. Faithful. Promiscuous. Tempted but faithful. Promiscuous in your hearts but faithful from feebleness.'[32] As in *The Common Pursuit*, there is no sense of self-righteousness or sanctimoniousness about this; the compulsion to break one's faith is universal, locked into the human organism like a virus, biding its time, waiting to assume control.

Bad faith as disease is also one of the themes of *Hidden Laughter*, Gray's most recent work for the theatre. In one scene Natalie describes how when she was a teenager she saw her father, Harry, with his secretary: 'There they were. *Really* at it. I could even see his erection. It was sticking up against his trousers. He looked sort of crazy. And now he's doing it with someone else, or possibly even someone else after the someone else.'[33] Like Humphry in *The Common Pursuit*, Natalie is scarred by the burden of comprehending things as they are. Her response is to reject her parents' self-righteous morality, declaring that her ambition is to 'Screw around, have a good time, shoot up in loos all over London, then get myself knocked up, live in a council house off state hand-outs, with three kids by different dads, that sort of thing.'[34] In a subsequent scene Harry reports that she is three months' pregnant: 'Though actually we don't see too much of her. She seems to feel that contact with us, even in the womb, might lead to it being contaminated in some way. Morally, I suppose she means.'[35] Harry prefers to put Natalie's rejection down to his being 'an English middle-class male' rather than accept the darker truth that he has become, as another character remarks, 'a bit of a joke. Peddling his wife's writings to compensate her for his infidelities. Which she doesn't seem to know about. Or care about.'[36] Harry is too much of a coward to confront such home truths; even in the final scene he tries to get the local clergyman, Ronnie, to explain to his wife Louise that he has finally decided to leave her:

> All I'm asking you to do as a man of God is to lessen the hurt for somebody you claim to care about. Why, I thought hurt-lessening was virtually all you believed in. The sum total of your faith. Two thousand years of Christian suffering – the virgin birth, the

crucifixion, martyrdoms, crusades, inquisitions, and here . . . here
. . . the climax of all that, the . . . the complete spiritual *climax* of
blood letting, suffering, death – a little English chap who believes
we shouldn't hurt people if we can help it. Or don't you believe
even that much, Ronnie?[37]

At which point Ronnie hurls himself furiously at Harry, crying out
'How dare you! How dare you!' Not only is this a grotesque
misrepresentation of his faith, but he resents the contempt implicit
in the argument that sexual infidelity is fine so long as you don't
hurt those who really love you. Not wanting to hurt anyone – a
defence repeated by nearly all Gray's sexual traitors – is offensive
because it is just a means of absolving oneself from blame. And in so
doing, it implies the opposite of what it pretends: a basic selfishness
that transcends one's compassion for the feelings of others.

In this respect Harry is no better than his father, Ben, who at first
suffers guilt when his behaviour leads, indirectly, to an accident in
which Harry's son Nigel is crippled when his leg is gored by a bull.
But Ben absolves himself when he tells Ronnie that

it gradually dawned on me, all this penance and pleading and
whining was a lot of nonsense. Self-pity. And what was worse,
arrogant. Yes, arrogant. I . . . I, little Benjamin Pertwee, take
responsibility! The sheer effrontery of it! Who am I to think I can
take responsibility for his decisions? Absolute bloody blasphemy,
when you think about it! Pardon my diplomatic language.
(*Laughs.*) But through all this I kept remembering what you'd
said – Emily asleep on Abraham's bosom. Do you see? (*Stares at
him intently.*) Emily. On Abraham's bosom. Yes. That's when it hit
me – slowly hit me, hit me very slowly – bong, bong, bong.
(*Thumps his head slowly but powerfully.*) . . . . What I do say is that if
we take God's view then there aren't any problems to solve.
They're all his problems, and he can solve them any way he wants
to, as long as we all end up on Abraham's bosom. There it is, in a
nutshell. Along with my thanks.[38]

Ronnie insists that 'there's been a bit of a . . . a misunderstanding
here. You see, I don't really think we can just shove all human
responsibility – *our* responsibility on to – '. He is interrupted when
Ben screams at the sight of Nigel's gored leg in a calliper,
undermining his exhaustive denial of responsibility more effectively than reasoned expostulation.

Because Ben and Harry remain oblivious to the sense of spirit observed by Ronnie in the speech with which I began, they refuse to deal honestly with themselves. Ricky Roma, one of the characters in David Mamet's *Glengarry Glen Ross* (1983), puts it bluntly: 'You think you're *queer* . . .? I'm going to tell you something: we're *all* queer. You think that you're a *thief*? So *what*? You get befuddled by a middle-class morality . . .? Get *shut* of it. Shut it out. You cheated on your wife . . .? You *did* it, *live* with it.'[39] Harry and Ben, like so many of Gray's characters, refuse to live with their actions, preferring to cover them up with bogus religiosity or moral posturing.

Ben's repeated reference to Abraham's bosom alludes to a poem in which this theme is uncomfortably close to home – too close for the comfort of its author. In 1802 Wordsworth met his illegitimate daughter, Caroline Vallon, for the first time. She was ten years old, and he undoubtedly felt a deep unease at the knowledge that he had abandoned her and her mother. After walking with her on the beach at Calais, he composed one of his most intriguing sonnets. Its assertion of peace and serenity suggests that the experience had allayed his guilt, which is further offset by the blessing bestowed on his child in the poem's closing lines. And yet, the thunder on the horizon indicates an inability to surrender to complacent self-justification:

> It is a beauteous Evening, calm and free;
> The holy time is quiet as a Nun
> Breathless with adoration; the broad sun
> Is sinking down in its tranquillity;
> The gentleness of heaven is on the Sea:
> Listen! the mighty Being is awake
> And doth with his eternal motion make
> A sound like thunder – everlastingly.
> Dear Child! Dear Girl! that walkest with me here,
> If thou appear'st untouched by solemn thought,
> Thy nature is not therefore less divine:
> Thou liest in Abraham's bosom all the year;
> And worshipp'st at the Temple's inner shrine,
> God being with thee when we know it not.

5

Howard Brenton:
Romantic Retreats

In 1972 Howard Brenton told Peter Ansorge that

> The theatre is a dirty place. It's not a place for a rational analysis
> of society – it's there to bait our obsessions, ideas and public
> figures.[1]

As this remark suggests, few British playwrights of the twentieth
century prior to Brenton and his occasional director and co-author,
David Hare, have so fully explored the implications of Artaud's
invitation, offered in the first manifesto to his 'Theatre of Cruelty', to
pursue 'a re-examination not only of all aspects of an objective,
descriptive outside world, but also all aspects of an inner world, that
is to say man viewed metaphysically, by every means at its
disposal.'[2] Like Artaud, Brenton is supremely romantic in his
conception of what theatre should be: he believes that the process of
inner and outer exploration should draw on the entire armoury of
theatrical effects. To him, the theatre is a kind of laboratory, in
which the object of experimentation is the audience. 'I challenge the
whole professional standard', Brenton told John Russell Taylor in
1970, 'it's done in panic . . . reasons of revenge, of hatred. . . . You
use any bit of old convention, any bit of old debris lying around and
smash it into it, and the subject matter becomes squeezed then, and
the meaning of what you're doing bleeds out.'[3] Such declarations,
with their unabashed insistence on preserving the passion of the
creative moment, are more relevant than ever to an age in which the
theatre has been cowed into formal conservativism.

Just how adventurous Brenton could be at this period is
confirmed by the psychodrama of *Christie In Love* (1970), in which
a victim of the mass murderer, John Christie, is played by an
inflatable doll whose words are spoken by a police constable.
Christie takes her home and gives her a cup of tea but there comes a
point at which he cannot continue with the reconstruction:

CHRISTIE: I have something on my mind. It comes back to me
   in flashes. If it does come back, I will tell you, I truly will.
   CHRISTIE *puts his hand between the* DOLL's *legs.*
CONSTABLE: Hello! I think he's off.
CHRISTIE: I don't remember what happened. But I must have
   gone haywire.[4]

Daringly, Brenton allows the mass-murderer to describe his frenzy
in the terms used by the early romantic poets to describe moments
of imaginative vision.[5] But he is neither attempting literary satire
nor aiming to ridicule Christie. In fact, Brenton is closer to his
romantic precursors than Christie's outrages may suggest;
Wordsworth's *Nutting* shows how emotional intensity can lead to
destruction. As Christie says, 'I don't remember what happened.
But I must have gone haywire.'

Brenton seeks not to justify murder, but his sympathies are with
the deep, informing passion that contrasts with the banal, stagnant
idea of love put forward by the Constable. 'Love's the bleeding
moon', the Constable remarks, 'And bleeding doves cooing. And
bleeding Frank Sinatra crooning. And holding hands. And a lovely
bunch of roses from the one whom you admire. . . . Not a corpse, in
a dirty garden.'[6] Debased, commercialised, deadened, the Constable's definition of feeling is the result of the repression of which
Christie's execution is the ultimate act. As the Inspector admits,
society has a vested interest in restricting the liberty of its citizens:
'What would happen if we all went right ahead, according to desire,
fucking all? Bleeding anarchy, Reg. Larceny, mutilation of animals,
murder.'[7] The Inspector must be right: the most stable societies are
the best controlled. But Brenton is not writing in support of state
indoctrination; in his view Christie is a martyr to the cause of
freedom, even if, on another level, he helps explain why revolutions
are too often betrayed into carnage.

Like the Constable, Jack, the ex-policeman of *Sore Throats* (1979), is
also guilty of repressing his feelings. 'Trouble with the English', he
confesses to his ex-wife Judy, 'we all go round with a Sunday-school
teacher in our heads. Some all-seeing do-gooder in the English brain
– stops us actually – breaking out. Going all the way.'[8] Jack's inner
conflict arises from the awareness that his failure to break out, to go
all the way, represents a spiritual betrayal. As such, it is more than
merely a question of psychology. He himself argues that our day-to-
day concern with material things stands in contradiction to love for

one's wife; as he puts it, 'not even a pig should be asked to fuck a Trustees Savings Bank Account!'

> In the last stages of my divorce, I had a bit of a fantasy. One night, driven mad by the mill of marriage and sex, I saw myself discovered by a fellow police-officer, outside a Trustees Savings Bank, my trousers and my Y-fronts down, my bum exposed to the night air and the fingers of passing drunks – with my cock jammed in a twenty-four-hour cash dispensing machine.
>
> Trying to reconcile money and sex.
>
> You've got to be free. Or you've got to feel free. That you do things freely. Or one thing, the best thing. Love.[9]

In spite of Jack's plea for an emotional and spiritual anarchy (or at least the semblance of it), he still needs money to emigrate to Canada with his girlfriend, Celia. If his situation echoes that of Brenton's father, also a disenchanted policeman, it is primarily by way of contrast. For while Brenton senior retired from the force to become a Methodist minister, Jack returns to Judy only to attack her violently and bloodily, forcing her to sign half their house over to him.

To regard *Sore Throats* on these grounds as a 'work of closet misogyny', as happened at the time of its first production,[10] is to misrepresent what is in fact a courageously undeceived view of human nature. When in 1988 the play was revived at the Royal Court Theatre as one of his '3 Plays for Utopia', Brenton insisted that 'if you are going to show people moving towards a transformation into citizens of a Utopia or, in SORE THROATS, a Utopian state of mind, you have to show them first at their vilest and their most unhappy.'[11] This is faithful both to psychology and politics, for the biggest incitement to revolution is the unhappiness produced by oppression; as the monster in Mary Shelley's *Frankenstein* puts it, 'Misery made me a fiend.'[12] In fact, Jack tastes freedom only when, stranded in the Canadian wilds, he has to deliver his girlfriend's child: 'Blood running in thin streams over the child, over the insides of her mother's legs and her father's hands.'[13]

For Brenton, liberation is a dirty, bloody, painful process. This is instinctively understood by Judy, whose desire to get guns and kill[14] is balanced by a visionary impulse: 'See a country, the other side of the wall. Sweet fields, rivers, forests. All you have to do is knock a few bricks out, wriggle through a hole onto the grass.'[15] Where Jack fails in his search for freedom and ends up wedded to the material world as a salesman of lavatory brushes, Judy draws strength from a sustaining optimism. The hole in the wall is a window onto a future that begins to crystallise even in the play's final moments, as she takes a lighted match to her remaining money, with the words: 'I am going to be fucked, happy and free.'[16]

The same line is uttered by Claire Clairmont in the second of Brenton's Plays for Utopia, *Bloody Poetry* (1984).[17] But if the second generation romantic poets travel further in their search for liberty, they are even more troubled than were Jack and Judy by the violent and destructive tendency of revolution. As Byron remarks, 'The world is bloody – and real – and we know it.'[18] Later he forces Shelley to recognise his own cruelty and negligence:

> Y'bloody hypocrite! Where is your legal wife? In England! The two women you are with, Mary y'call your wife, Claire y'friend – concubines, sir! Y'mistresses, sir! All your idealism, revolution in society, revolution in the personal life, all trumpery! The practice of it, sir, the practice doth make us dirty, doth make all naked and bleeding and real!
> *Angry.*
> Y'damn theorising! All you want to do is get your end away. And you make bloody sure you do![19]

If Brenton makes no attempt to discredit Byron's cynicism, he allows Shelley also to ridicule Byron:

> . . . for a poet to despair? Obscene! We claim to be the poets of the people of England. How dare we – luxuriate in denouncing the human cause as lost?
> The great instrument of moral good is the imagination. We must not let it become diseased! We must be optimists for human nature![20]

Bloody Poetry confronts the extremes represented by Shelley and Byron so as to suggest that either on its own results, at best, in heroic failure. The play's final image is of Shelley's funeral pyre, as envisaged by Byron: 'Burn him! Burn him! Burn him! Burn us all! A great big, bloody, beautiful fire!'[21] But this is less a critique than a celebration of the optimism advocated by Shelley. The glory of their failure resides, Brenton argues, in the mere fact of their daring to experiment with alternative social and political configurations. Claire Clairmont, the most driven of them, declares that 'we will become magnificent. The men and women of the future will thank us. We are their great experiment. We will find out how to live and love, without fear.'[22] Despite the apparent failure of their lives, Brenton reserves judgment on their aspirations; as he observes in the programme note for his 'Plays for Utopia': 'Whether they really failed in their "Utopian dreams" is not yet resolved.'

The third of the Utopian plays, *Greenland* (1988), is a fantasy which attempts to resolve that question by projecting it into a future in which the ideals of the romantics are realised. Set on Election Night in 1987, it deplores a world in which the proletariat would rather watch *EastEnders* than vote Labour, and where the closest we can get to our ideals is through a dirty weekend in Brighton. As an antidote to political defeat Brenton offers us Greenland in which, 700 years in the future, people live and love freely. At which point, as Brenton was aware, the drama breaks down. Stripped of conflict and struggle, life in its idealised form becomes predictable and dull – symptomatic of which is the fact that the most interesting of the Greenlanders is the last reactionary, Severan-Severan:

> Damn passivity! Is the dialectic at rest forever? What is at war with what? Peace is senility, worst in the young! Is human nature now a mere mirror to itself? There are people now abroad who believe that human nature is changed, for the good, forever. Bunk! There is a worm in man .... In the end we are all selfish, self-obsessed, with a dark heart. Human nature? It is evil and it will out.[23]

As the direct descendant of Byron in *Bloody Poetry*, Severan is the play's sole redeeming element. He also provides its only comic moment: 'Give me something to fight against, give me anguish, give me struggle!', he screams, 'I think I'll break my arm! Someone, break my arm for me!' If a dictatorship takes the form of universal benevolence, revolutionary behaviour must liberate evil, even if that means inflicting it on oneself. The moral determinism of *Greenland* provides Severan with ample reason for describing it as a 'living death',[24] thereby allowing Brenton to renege on the promise made in his 1988 programme note to 'come clean' about his ideal world. *Greenland* does nothing of the sort; it is a fantasy, a conceit, a romantic possibility exposing the dangers of idealising human nature.

In fact, despite the prominence Brenton has given to the utopian tendencies in his work, they are really the by-product of a more pervasive scepticism. Like *Greenland*, *Thirteenth Night* (1981) is a political fantasy but one more representative of his thinking. Written in the wake of the 1979 election defeat, it postulates a near future in which the Labour Party takes power. What might be a utopian play along similar lines as *Greenland* turns into a nightmare in which the career of the Labour Prime Minister, Jack Beaty, parallels that of Macbeth. While on one hand he preaches 'a new democracy, new forms, a politics to end politics', on the other he excuses his colleagues' executions with the thought that 'If good comes of it, the dead are forgotten.'[25] His assumption that the ends justify the means is both complacent and untrue: in Beaty's case the means represent a betrayal of the ends.

Discussing *Thirteenth Night*, Brenton declared that 'I get sick of plays about the left, which do not mention the basic socialist problem. I mean – the blood in the Revolution's cradle.'[26] Brenton is too much of an optimist to blame this purely on 'the worm in man', and the lurking anxiety of much of his 1980s work is that evil is latent in the idealising process. *The Genius* (1983) is a kind of political parable in which a gifted young mathematician, Leo Lehrer, makes a major discovery that he realises will be used to make weapons of mass destruction. Unlike Einstein, Leo doesn't believe in God, but nevertheless feels obliged to conceal his work for fear of its consequences:

> I feel like a singer, who sings a note in innocence and all the glass in the windows smashes. Is the consequence of what I think down to me or not? I say – not. I am sick of being some kind of moralist by default – all because I was in love with numbers.[27]

It may be true, as Leo suggests, that action, however well-intentioned, is inherently corrupting, but that hardly justifies the distinction he posits between thought and action. Some kind of distinction may be possible but it is not of the kind by which thinkers may be absolved from responsibility for the actions they inspire. In Brenton's translation of Brecht's *The Life of Galileo* (1980), Galileo admits that, although he has handed the fruits of his knowledge over to the authorities, 'a new age has dawned'.[28]

Similarly, when Leo Lehrer hands his work over to the intelligence services, he sets in train a series of events implied by the discovery itself. The revelation granted by his experience is that the 'worm in man' is inherent in all intellectual activity; as Leo puts it,

> The ideas do not love us. I have come to the conclusion that all the investigations into the atom, discoveries, calculations, formulations, nearer and nearer to the description of the force of nature – the scientific quest of the century – is fundamentally malign. . . . Malignity! In the ideas, in the idea of the ideas. If I were religious – and thank the fuck I'm not – I'd start talking about evil.[29]

Leo's insight is not confined to scientific discourse. Brenton's avowed horror at the blood in the cradle of revolution extends his argument into the political arena. His most searching discussion of this occurs in *H.I.D. (Hess is Dead)* (1989), in which two academic Marxist historians, Nicole and Raymond, conspire in a cover-up of the murder of Rudolph Hess. Nicole reassures herself with the thought that 'Reality is salmonella', a poison from which the world needs protection: 'So cook the news.'[30] She is justified in view of the fact that were it to become known that the authorities had killed Hess rather than that he had committed suicide it could spark off a wave of nationalist violence in Germany. But when Nicole remarks,

> To market
> history
> remove
> Impurities
> add harmless
> sweeteners[31]

she is betrayed by her language. The 'marketing' of history, however laudable its aim, must compromise her Marxist ideals. The instigator of the cover-up is a man called Luber who is dying and addresses them only on video. He observes to Raymond that, just

> as your weltanschauung failed, your world view, the Marxist millennium, so has my stomach . . . It is the oyster in the shell that has done for me . . . where does the drive to human wholeness lead? Like Galileo, to grossness, obscenity, obsession . . . . An

intellectual passion to understand the world, can what? Become a desire to eat the world? That is my fate, my dear colleagues, to degenerate to gluttony. With me it is oysters . . . Fragments of shells have perforated my intestine . . .[32]

Luber's strange, disconnected address is a chilling denunciation of intellectual process. Beginning with the observation that its best fruits, such as a Marxist millennium, have failed to materialise, he suggests that far from helping worthy causes it is self-serving and self-edifying, like the consumption of oysters. At the same time, like the oyster's shell, it can betray us in the most horrible manner. 'We are morticians', he continues, 'we deliver history with an acceptable face . . . acceptable facts, which may or may not be true . . . but they are safe . . . to be taught on the Modern History exam syllabus . . .'[33] Nicole and Raymond realise too late that by producing a fiction in which reality has been quietly put to sleep they have further thwarted the Marxist principles they espouse.

In his only novel, *Diving for Pearls* (1989) Brenton continues this discussion with a detailed account of the pervasive sense of outrage and ideological betrayal felt by socialists during the Thatcher years. Having rejected her upper class origins in favour of a modish but dedicated radicalism, its protagonist, Cecily Rose, has betrayed her class before the novel begins. She goes on to forfeit even her political credentials by falling in love with a convicted criminal, Frank Blake, who works part-time as a double agent for both British Intelligence and the IRA. These telescoping, spiralling infidelities lead to a bloody dénouement when a former army officer, Peter Carter, whom Frank betrayed to republican snipers, hunts them down. 'You know, Cecily', Peter tells her, with cold accuracy, 'In your heart, you know what he is . . .'[34] Like it or not, Brenton confronts the liberal conscience with the unpalatable fact that treachery is potential in every committed act, even those of love.

The numbing inevitability with which these conclusions unravel might have produced a highly pessimistic work. But *Diving for Pearls* refuses to admit defeat, remaining uneasily poised between hope and despair.[35] Even at an early stage Cecily 'had to face the fact that her renegade instincts, her obscure and inarticulate drive to some personal insurrection, which she could not explain even to herself, were those of an incurable romantic.'[36] But it would be a mistake to conclude that Brenton retreats to a moral high ground in her defence; instead he asks whether the rot at the heart of all beliefs might be the source of strength rather than weakness. In Shakespeare's play, the death of King Lear is eased by the delusion that Cordelia still lives; his final words are: 'Look her lips,/ Look there, look there!'[37] By the same token Cecily's love for Frank gives her the strength not merely to face their joint deaths, but to arrange with Carter where and when they will occur. Perhaps their love is inherently flawed, perhaps it is the product of multiple, concentric infidelities – but it is sufficiently strong to withstand Frank's acceptance of Cecily's tip-off to Carter. 'It don't matter, love. It don't matter at all', are his last words. When they have been murdered, a friend tells Cecily's sister: 'Not to be so sad. . . . They had much fun. . . . Romantisch. They were romantic.'[38]

Those who find this illogical and inconclusive might reflect that these are the very qualities that make the novel so effective. But it would be a mistake to argue that Brenton's conclusion is in any way pat. After all, it is overshadowed by the same sense of loss, degradation, and falsehood that suffuses even the novel's deepest recesses. This is reflected in its evocation of Thatcher's Britain, of which it is, along with Ian McEwan's *The Child in Time*, one of the most grimly accurate:

> It was the surfaces of things that made her wince, a gold Rolex watch on the wrist of a twenty-four year-old, drunk in a city wine bar, or, on the television news one night, the mother of a twelve-year-old girl who had been abducted being asked by the interviewer, 'How do you feel about the man who did this?', then the tear-clotted eyes gone and news about a golf-tournament on the screen . . . and how women were once again in high heels in the streets, with their calves stretched, put back into tight clothing after the wear-anything spirit of the 1970s . . . by something that was happening to the country that was demeaning, making everything mean, making surfaces nasty.[39]

The novel's oppressive, insatiable accumulation of 1980s trash, including the 'cheap Italian red and cans of Carlsberg Special Brew' in Cecily's flat, her Kodak disk camera, and 'immaculately pumiced jeans',[40] reminds us that our ideology is conditioned and contaminated by the very environment in which we have our being. But on a technical level too, this hunger for substance, the desire to incorporate the raw matter of everyday life into the linguistic texture of his prose, suggests a corresponding dislike of artifice. In fact, *Diving for Pearls* raises an important question about the nature of the fictionalising process. As I have noted, the retreat to romanticism in the novel's closing pages is calculatedly ambiguous. By invoking the delusions of Lear it succeeds on a poetic level in heightening our tragic sense of waste. But just as Cordelia must, despite her innocence, be executed, so too must the forces of corruption overwhelm Brenton's protagonists. If Brenton remains, like Shelley, an optimist for human nature, that optimism seems in the work of the late 1980s and early 1990s to be increasingly tested, even reserved. It is in this spirit that he fastens his invented characters to the grit-impacted surfaces of 1980s Britain, for if the fiction is to have any relevance at all to our lives, the gap between the outside world and our idealising tendencies must be closed.

This dilemma is illustrated in *Hess is Dead*, where the fiction concocted by Nicole and Raymond obscures the truth about Hess's death, but fails to suppress the fascism latent in the human organism. In the play's final scene the walls of Spandau prison warn us that although 'the old lies / Are forgotten', and the prison itself has been razed to the ground,

> We are in you
>   and will rise again
>   we are cancer, we are there
> We will be
>   revenged
>   and rise again.[41]

Such malignancy casts doubt over Cecily's recourse to romanticism and begs the question of whether qualitative distinctions can be made between the marketing of lies and the writing of plays. Clues may be found in the neurotic accretion of detail in *Diving for Pearls*, as well as in Nicole's CV, which lists a defence of cultural terrorism.

Brenton's response arose from his collaboration with Tariq Ali on *Iranian Nights*, a short play inspired by the *fatwa* issued by the Ayatollah Khomeini against the novelist Salman Rushdie. Brenton introduces the published text as 'a pinprick for free speech',[42] and it indeed addresses the issues raised by the Rushdie affair. But its approach is oblique: the play contains none of the contemporary figures involved, and makes no attempt to dramatise their actions. Brenton and Ali's next joint work, *Moscow Gold* (1990), was more audacious; it aims to follow Meyerhold in its creation of 'living history', a theatre 'plugged directly into reality', presenting exactly 'what people were really thinking and doing' at precise historical moments.[43] If this is not quite cultural terrorism it is a valiant attempt to make the decisions made by contemporary political figures vital and immediate, cutting through the fictionalising tendency inherent in reportage.

Its protagonist, Mikhail Gorbachev, remains optimistic, confessing to a 'faith that people can be reclaimed',[44] but he is confronted by the overwhelming forces of history. 'It's a sad business', he tells Raisa, 'making history under circumstances out of your control . . .'[45] This doomed struggle distances the Soviet Union even further from the ideals out of which it was born. As if to emphasize this, the play begins with the image of Lenin, centre stage, announcing: 'We will now proceed to construct the socialist order.'[46] No less compelling than any other romantic aspiration, the socialist order nevertheless degenerates into a bloody nightmare of treachery and double-dealing.

The play has two endings: one envisaging the worst (Gorbachev's assassination by the forces of conservativism), the other taking a more hopeful view. In old age, Gorbachev and Raisa sit on the verandah of their autumn dacha and read the news.

GORBACHEV: The news is bad. The Americans are in trouble.
    They're desperately short of wheat this year. Want our help.
RAISA: No! Their human rights record last year was atrocious!
GORBACHEV: Yes. But. (*He shrugs.*) The Soviet Union does not
    want the American people to be without bread.[47]

By reversing the situation of the 1990s, so that it is the West rather than the East where food is in short supply, and the Americans whose human rights record is at fault, Brenton and Ali spotlight the meanness of our response to the Russians' current plight. All of which is given emphasis by the reminder that popular unrest at material deprivation contributed in large part to Gorbachev's downfall. But Gorbachev's ungrudging liberality in the face of such uneasy reflections indicates that the play's politics are morally founded. In the real world, the play suggests, where our aspirations are hedged about by practicalities, it may be that the most we can demonstrate towards others is the same generosity of spirit Gorbachev shows towards America. 'There is an infinite variety of ways of making theatre', Brenton has remarked, 'but only one theme which, inevitably, Aeschylus was onto – it's simply "how can we live justly?"'[48] Within the play, Gorbachev tries to implement this moral imperative, and to reassert Lenin's socialist order, by shifting power from the apparatchiks to the people: 'We must keep control. Human beings must be at the centre of our society, we must have social justice.'[49] If at first hearing that sounds rather attenuated beside Shelley's visionary utterances in *Bloody Poetry*, it should be remembered that the attempt to turn 'a decayed, authoritarian system' such as the Soviet Union into a 'commonwealth of nations with a new, democratic socialism',[50] was in 1990 a highly optimistic prospect – just think how futile such hopes seem now. That sense of futility is confronted in Brenton's most recent work, *Berlin Bertie* (1992).

To recapitulate: in *Diving for Pearls* Brenton refuses to resolve the ambiguous status of romanticism in Cecily's thinking. It makes her happy, but it is also leads to self-destruction. That ambiguity is allowed to cast doubt over the entire creative process in *H.I.D.*, where marketing of any kind is regarded as a corrupting influence. This is hardly resolved in *Moscow Gold*, where idealism is grounded in the palpable reality of Soviet politics, and where its highest expression is a plea for justice. In his grimmest moments Brenton has conceived of failure only at arm's length, as in *Thirteenth Night*, where it occurs within the framework of a dystopian fantasy designed to give left-wing activists a cautionary nudge.

Berlin Bertie moves into even darker territory, for it comprehends failure as a reality, incorporating it into the psychology of its protagonists and the physical structure of its environment. It is set in a decaying council flat in South London rented by Alice, a social worker suspended after the beating to death of Kylie, a baby under her care. 'I mean', she tells her sister Rosa, 'this BLOKE burnt his baby on an electric fire, beat her head against the wall then bit her to wake her up when she was dead .... this is just FUCKING HUMANITY getting on with everyday life'.[51] Alice's cynicism is neither qualified nor undermined; contemporary Britain as she describes it is gripped by a disease of which acts of violence are a symptom.

Though young, her boyfriend Sandy is a far cry from the male odalisque dreamed up by Judy in *Sore Throats*;[52] when Rosa suggests that he is living off her sister, he throws the ironing board across the room:

ROSA: Sandy, don't smash things.
SANDY: You fucking talking to me?
ROSA: . . . . It's repetitious behaviour, it's a pattern . . .[53]

As a psychiatrist Rosa is well-qualified to diagnose psychological disorders, and, as it turns out, she has written a thesis on swearing that probably theorizes about the language Sandy uses. Be this as it may, the cure lies beyond her reach, just as her sister was powerless to prevent Kylie's death. In the post-Thatcher era, that cancerous force embedded deep in the walls of Spandau prison has finally triumphed. The liberal education which was once the cornerstone of social justice – and which, as we have seen, was the means by which the Marxist historians of *H.I.D.* betrayed themselves – can help no one. Indeed, it is not only devalued but mocked. When Rosa and Alice accuse Sandy of ignorance he responds: 'I tell you clever-clever cows, I know what I fucking need to know and I fucking get by on it. Can you two say that? Do you know what you need to know? Do you get by on it? The fuck you do.'[54] Foul-mouthed, complacent, self-righteous, Sandy is also correct. For the vast majority of people life continues at the level of basic survival for which university degrees in, say, English literature, are useless.

But this is a story not merely of cultural breakdown. In more optimistic times Alice's sister Rosa emigrated to East Berlin where she became a Christian and married a priest: 'I wanted to go forth into the world shining, with a fresh UPWARD look on my face.'[55] Since her political and religious views were inextricably related, the passing of her faith has not left her idealism untouched:

To suddenly see Creation . . . not as from God's hand, but as a horrific kind of . . . entity. A huge amoeba . . . of meaningless life, with its slime everywhere, on everything, on your thoughts, even on things, your clothes, the food you eat . . . you cannot possibly have any idea of the disgust.[56]

The romantic vision transforms. It depends on our belief in our ability to change things for the better; as Shelley puts it in *Bloody Poetry*, 'The great instrument of moral good is the imagination.'[57] Rosa's disgust arises from her inability to see beyond the rancid materiality of things, or to comprehend physical existence as anything but an end in itself.

Beginning with Coleridge's *Dejection* the failure of vision has become as much a staple of romantic myth-making as its triumph; Berlin Bertie, a former Stasi agent who calls himself Bertolt Brecht, and who spied on Rosa and her husband, Joachim, is the means by which that failure is contextualised. Back in East Berlin he showed Rosa a file in which Joachim was named as a double agent. It may be symptomatic of Brenton's own changing attitudes that where a similar disclosure intensified Cecily's love for Frank in *Diving for Pearls*, it leads to Rosa's desertion of Joachim. When Bertie catches up with her in South London, he tells her that the files were doctored, that it is impossible to tell 'forged reports from innocents . . . jumbled up with the real "Judases"'.[58] Whether or not Joachim was a double agent, Rosa realises that she is the real Judas of the play: 'I trusted a bit of paper, not the man. Now the bit of paper itself, can't be trusted.'[59] With that betrayal the last shreds of moral certainty are stripped away, and she surrenders herself to the new world of the post-communist era in which nothing can be differentiated. One of Bertie's plans is to sell pirated video games from Eastern Europe to the West:

> There is a video game. It's German. The game is called 'Aryan Test'. Players become concentration camp managers, they have to spot who is a Jew who is not, prevent mass escape etcetera. The game contravenes laws forbidding the propagation of hatred, but the police cannot track down its makers. (*He smiles.*) By next Easter, I could be a millionaire. A materialist salvation at least, Rosa.[60]

Bertie's use of 'salvation' is calculatedly ironic, as is the prospect that he might next celebrate Christ's crucifixion with his first million. If this is a mockery of spiritual values it has an abundance of meaning if you happen to live in a decayed council flat in South London. But that's the least of it. In the utopian fancies of the English Romantics moral good was a necessary force for social improvement. By contrast, the huge amoeba of life by which Rosa is surrounded in her apostasy is meaningless and horrifyingly undifferentiated. She has betrayed herself to a world contemptuous of moral distinction, of which Bertie is both spokesman and exploiter. Extremes of human suffering which once provided a basis for the construction of behavioural codes are now so demeaned that video games like 'Aryan Test' can make him his fortune. The very idea of a holocaust industry might be regarded as obscene were it not for the fact that repugnance on moral grounds is no longer possible, since value judgements are determined not by abstract ideals but by how much money you, I or it makes.

Brenton's account of bad faith and secular despair is extended by Joanne, a homeless 17-year-old to whom Alice gives shelter, whose ambition is to travel across Europe doing a mime show about the end of the world. When Alice reveals this to Rosa she warns her not to say the obvious:

> DON'T SAY what right has this kid got, with a nose . . . clown's nose on a rubber band over her face, to thumb a lift, from a lorry driver with a load of Euro lamb, by the turn off to Belsen Belsen . . . . DON'T SAY doesn't she know she's flitting through RUBBLE, don't say doesn't she know she's being arty, across a continent that's . . . that's a tacky, built-up area, McDonald's and holiday homes over a SMASHED-UP GRAVEYARD, don't say doesn't she realise her stupid little mime . . . is an insult to millions who have suffered all too recently, yourself included, in your way, sister mine, DON'T SAY IT . . .[61]

As Alice's refrain suggests, the contempt implied by Joanne's little project is the product of ignorance rather than inhumanity. This cuts both ways, since on one hand ignorance is no justification and in some respects makes Joanne even more culpable. However, what little hope the play scrapes together is concentrated in an absence of malice which, it seems to suggest, is the best to be expected from human nature in the final decade of the twentieth century. 'What could be more despicable than you and I?' Rosa asks her sister, 'We wanted to put the world to rights. . . . But we're despicable, we're the lowest of the low, because we failed . . . So what shall we do? Make a penance? Go and eat earth? In a London park? Boil STONES for supper?'[62] Significantly, Joanne is the only character with an answer:

> Turn a strange corner
> > arch your back
> And SLIP in through
>
> Open a door in the air
> > free
> Human flight

> It's in us
> > I know
> It's a KNACK
>
> All you've got to do
> > is just
> Slip through[63]

If the sense of defeat is stronger in *Berlin Bertie* than in Brenton's earlier work, hope is still attributable to the young, even if they no longer have a conscience. The cynical response might be to accuse Brenton of sentimentality, but to have denied us a 'door in the air' would have been selfish. Cynicism is a disease, leaving resistance as the only course for a truly moral writer. Consider Lawrence's *Apocalypse*, in which he insists even in the face of his own death how foolish we are for divesting ourselves 'of [our] emotional and imaginative reactions, and feeling nothing'.[64] Or, more recently, Primo Levi, a survivor of Auschwitz who, a year before his death, remarked: 'You may be certain that the world is heading for destruction, but it's a good thing, a moral thing, to behave as though there's still hope. Hope is as contagious as despair: your hope, or show of hope, is a gift you can give to your neighbour, and may even help to prevent or delay the destruction of his world.'[65]

6

David Hare: A Milder Day

'I am a man on a moral mission. I want people to see life as it is. I want them to see their real situation. . . . See things as they really are. To everyone I pose a question. I am the question.'[1] What might be a plausible alibi for any politically correct playwright of the 1990s is, in the mouth of Lambert Le Roux, the corrupt newspaper baron of *Pravda* (1985), a declaration of ethical bad faith. Le Roux's aim, to divest people of their ideals, can bear only a parodic relation to that of the play's authors, Howard Brenton and David Hare. And yet, as we saw in the previous chapter, Brenton's most recent plays are marked by a deep scepticism about the very nature of principled behaviour; I'd like to begin this discussion of David Hare by tracing the same anxiety in his work.

Susan Traherne, the protagonist of *Plenty* (1978), is a spiritual extremist whose strength derives from her wartime experiences when, as she recalls, 'You believed in the organization. You had to. If you didn't, you would die.'[2] In particular, she is haunted by a brief encounter with an undercover agent called Lazar, who parachuted into the French village where she was stationed during the German occupation.

> LAZAR: Come on, let's clear this lot up. We must be off. I don't know how I'm going to manage on French cigarettes. Is there somewhere I can buy bicycle clips? I was thinking about it all the way down. Oh yes and something else. A mackerel sky. What is the phrase for that?
> SUSAN: Un ciel pommelé.
> LAZAR: Un ciel pommelé. Marvellous. I must find a place to slip it in. Now. Where will I find this bike?[3]

The mackerel sky pulls us, as it does Susan, out of the temporal moment into sublimity. Its vividness and intensity derives from the fact that it is imaginatively and emotionally prejudiced, attached to the tension and suppressed eroticism of the encounter with Lazar. And, like the strength of her belief in the organisation for which she works, its intangibility endows it with an almost religious power. That fragile, timeless experience informs the beliefs that are to shape her life. In the final scene, which returns to her wartime experiences, she encounters a Frenchman who observes that the English hide their feelings. But, she tells him, 'things will quickly change. We have grown up. We will improve our world. . . . There will be days and days and days like this.'[4]

The prospect of a better world extends beyond time into a millennial future, but as in the final scene of Simon Gray's *The Common Pursuit* the play's emotional charge arises out of the thwarting of that aspiration by subsequent events. For postwar England, as seen in the play, remains as emotionally straitjacketed as, for instance, Marcia, the librarian of *Wetherby* who works in a building surrounded by barbed wire. When Susan meets her husband's boss at the Foreign Office, Sir Andrew Charleson, he tells her that

> That is the nature of the service, Mrs Brock. It is called diplomacy. And in its practice the English lead the world. (*He smiles.*) The irony is this: we had an empire to administer, there were six hundred of us in this place. Now it's to be dismantled and there are six thousand. As our power declines, the fight among us for access to that power becomes a little more urgent, a little uglier perhaps. As our influence wanes, as our empire collapses, there is little to believe in. Behaviour is all.[5]

Charleson sets the historical context: an empire in decline finds the Roman virtues of grace, sociability, and forbearance more compelling than truth to the emotions. It is symptomatic that when Susan tells him that if her husband 'is not promoted in the next six days, I am intending to shoot myself', she is dragged screaming from the room and taken 'to the surgery'.[6] Her violation of a moral code that values restraint above all else is evidence of her refusal to abandon her beliefs; as Hare admits, 'What drives Susan mad is that society doesn't offer any good way to live. *Plenty* is about the cost of a life spent in dissent'.[7] The virtue of Susan's position is taken for granted; what concerns Hare most is the uneasy paradox that fidelity to high ideals can destroy our lives. Despite her threats, Susan never does shoot herself, but she is responsible for some brutally insensitive acts. It is significant that Kate Nelligan, who first created the role, confesses that 'I stopped admiring the woman. I really wanted to pummel her. I would come to the middle of the second act, and I would just withdraw my consent from that woman. I don't think the audience ever knew, but I was very worried about it.'[8]

Susan's most articulate critic is her wretched husband Raymond, whose career she helps to ruin. Just before she walks out on him he tells her that

> Your life is selfish, self-interested gain. That's the most charitable interpretation to hand. You claim to be protecting some personal ideal, always at a cost of almost infinite pain to everyone around you. You are selfish, brutish, unkind. Jealous of other people's happiness as well, determined to destroy other ways of happiness they find. I've spent fifteen years of my life trying to help you, simply trying to be kind, and my great comfort has been that I am waiting for some indication from you . . . some sign that you have valued this kindness of mine. Some love perhaps.[9]

By any objective standards he is right. Her admission that 'I like to lose control'[10] is borne out by her outburst in Charleson's office and by her shooting of Mick, a former boyfriend. As she recalls, it was Raymond's bribery that silenced him: 'It was after Raymond's kindness I felt I had to get engaged . . .'[11] But Raymond is deceived if he hopes that obligation will give way to love, as its only lasting result is to deepen her sense of betrayal. He is, after all, representative of postwar Britain's moral malaise, favouring, for example, the licensed insincerity of Foreign Service ethics: 'Hypocrisy does keep things pleasant for at least part of the time.'[12]

Susan refuses to compromise her beliefs but rather than shoot herself she attempts to reclaim the past. Realising that wartime austerity brought her closer to people she sheds her possessions: 'I've stripped away everything, everything I've known. There's only one kind of dignity, that's in living alone. The clothes you stand up in, the world you can see . . .'[13] Twenty years after their first encounter she sleeps with Lazar in a cheap hotel where they make love in their overcoats. If this is a triumph of the will it stops well short of the millenarian expectation of 'days and days and days like this'. In the face of such failure, reconstruction of the past is her sole consolation.

Wetherby (1985), Hare's first feature film, is far less remitting in its critique. It concerns the relationship between a postgraduate

student, John Morgan, and a middle-aged schoolteacher, Jean
Travers, whose dinner party he gatecrashes. During the party he
is asked what he makes of other people:

> MORGAN: Well, I don't know. I only know goodness and anger
> and revenge and evil and desire . . . these seem to me far
> better words than neurosis and psychology and paranoia.
> These old words . . . these good old words have a sort of
> conviction which all this modern apparatus of language now
> lacks.
> (*People have stopped eating and are looking at him. There is a silence.*)
> MARCIA: Ah, well, yes . . .
> MORGAN: We bury these words, these simple feelings, we bury
> them deep. And all the building over that constitutes this
> century will not wish these feelings away.
> (*There is a pause. JEAN looks at him. He looks steadily back.*)
> ROGER: Well, I mean, you'd have to say what you really mean
> by that.
> MORGAN: Would I?
> ROGER: Define your terms.
> (MORGAN *looks at him.*)
> MORGAN: They don't need defining. If you can't feel them you
> might as well be dead.[14]

Morgan embarrasses the guests at Jean's party by speaking of
passions they have long since repressed. Against the intellected
'apparatus' invoked as a kind of emotional anaesthetic he prefers
'good old words' like 'goodness and anger and revenge and evil and
desire' – terms reminiscent of Biblical teachings. Like an Old
Testament prophet, his random encounters give rise to both
extraordinary insights and seeming acts of lunacy. For all his
wisdom, it is he who returns to Jean the next day, puts a gun to his
mouth, and blows his brains out. Such obscenity has its own logic,
for he is cursed with a profound awareness of what Lambert Le
Roux calls 'life as it is'. It is through his eyes that we see the barbed
wire surrounding the library in which Jean's best friend Marcia
works, and through his eyes that we see his workplace, the
University of Essex: 'A gulch of tower blocks. They stand, lined
up, sinister, desolated. Scraps of paper blow down between them. A
scene more like urban desolation than a university.'[15] As Verity, one

of Jean's other friends, remarks, 'Life is *dangerous*. Don't you realise? And sometimes there's nothing you can do.'[16] Morgan parts company with her in his belief that something *can* be done. Just as, perched on the tops of mountains, Wordsworth's Pedlar felt 'sensation, soul and form'[17] melt into him, Morgan craves a similar sense of unity and completion. Or, as Hare puts it, Morgan is 'an emotional junkie who'd do anything for a sensation'.[18] 'I want some feeling! I want some contact! I want you fucking near me!' he screams at Karen, one of the other students at Essex. Karen's rejection of him, Jean realises, 'drove Morgan crazy',[19] plunging him into an infernal isolation from which there is only one escape.

A full understanding of his suicide is denied Jean until she confesses to the policeman, Langdon, everything that took place on the night of her dinner party. She recalls that when one of the tiles blew off the the roof Morgan volunteered to repair it. She went up with him into the roof but before they went back down she seized him. They clutched at each other and he pulled her down to the floor.

MORGAN: You and I – we understand each other.
JEAN: What? No . . . what?
MORGAN: You fake. You fake all that cheerfulness.
JEAN: No, please. It's who I am.
MORGAN: They why did you lead me up here?
JEAN: I didn't.
MORGAN: Liar! (*He twists her head and speaks into her ear.*) You
    know. You know where you're looking.
JEAN: I don't.
MORGAN: You've been here. Where I am.[20]

Morgan recognises that Jean shares the tortured inner state for which the desolation of Essex University provides an objective correlative. Having discovered a fellow inhabitant of his own hell Morgan seals their affinity forever by sharing with her the most intimate act he could commit. On one level the blowing-off of his head parodies the mystic enlightenment that led, for the romantics, to a greater love of humanity,[21] but such easy parallels belie the complexity of the emotional drama.

'You've been here', Morgan tells Jean, 'Where I am.' And as he lifts the revolver to his mouth he recalls his arrival at her dinner party, his last utterance being that 'you accepted me'.[22] Jean is complicit, more so than she at first realises, in Morgan's suicide. The film's real subject is her acceptance that Morgan was an extreme version of herself, that the sensitivity that makes her such a good teacher gives her the same destructive potential.

Wetherby, Hare's most searching discussion of the nature of good intentions, dates back to 1985, since when he has returned only once to the subject, in the feature film *Strapless* (1989). As its title suggests, *Strapless* is a more exuberant outing. Its hero, Raymond, is less destructive than Susan and Morgan, and his extreme hunger for romance is faintly ridiculous. As his first wife says, 'he couldn't just live. Just *live*. Just be. . . . He wanted permanent romance.'[23] And when he deserts Lillian, the NHS doctor he has bigamously married, she realises that he has taught her something: 'I've been very arrogant', Lillian tells her sister, Amy, 'I thought I was exempt. No one's exempt. You have certain feelings. And then you must pick up the bill.'[24] As in *Wetherby*, an encounter with a spiritual extremist forces the protagonist to confront the nature of her own romantic impulses.

But for all that, *Strapless* moves in a different direction from its predecessors, for *Plenty* and *Wetherby* are essentially tragic. In *King Lear*, which Hare directed at the National Theatre in 1986, Lear's supreme hope at the end of the play is that his relationship with Cordelia transcends the dealings of the world and is immortal:

> we'll wear out,
> In a wall'd prison, packs and sects of great ones,
> That ebb and flow by th' moon.[25]

The play's emotional crux turns on the fact not that he is wrong but that his aspirations must be confronted – in the space of seven lines, in fact – with a reality in which Cordelia must be hanged. Lear survives only long enough to ask 'Why should a dog, a horse, a rat, have life,/And thou no breath at all?'[26] Such disparities constitute a tragic sense of life that is shared by Susan in *Plenty* and Morgan in *Wetherby*; against the odds, they defy the repression and inhumanity around them even if it means self-destruction.

Significantly, the same cannot be said of Raymond in *Strapless*, who is simply a rogue – feckless, capricious, and, like the film itself, comic. This is symptomatic of a larger shift of feeling in Hare's work during the late 1980s. Where Brenton has become increasingly preoccupied by doubt, Hare has moved in the opposite direction.

His view of idealism may carry a cautionary element, embodied by characters like Susan, Morgan and (perhaps) Raymond, but the effect of the Thatcher years has been to make him more assured of its value. Where Brenton's revolutionaries have all turned traitor in the 1990s, Hare's have drawn strength from the faithlessness in society at large. Picking up the bill, as Lillian puts it, means resisting infidelity of all kinds, whether that means truth to one's emotions, or resisting the erosion of political or moral principles one knows to be just. Thus, having recognised that no one is exempt, Lillian agrees to represent the doctors in her hospital who wish to defend the health service against the government.

Leonard, the poet of Hare's most recent television play, *Heading Home* (1991), set in 1947, inhabits the same trusting world that sustained Susan during her wartime experience. As his friend Beryl explains to his new girlfriend Janetta, 'part of the fun is, things don't need saying. Isn't that what friendship is about? You don't have to say anything. And yet things are understood between you.'[27] Wordsworth's millennial theories postulated a language that transcended the spoken word, untroubled by the fallibility of verbal construction, and rooted directly in our emotions;[28] Leonard and Beryl have acquired that tongue by their very closeness. In fact Leonard has invested himself in a poetic discourse that aspires to the same sublime ends. When he and Janetta go to the beach he tries to explain why, by reference to his wartime experience.

LEONARD: When you're going down, it's as if in slow motion. You can see the torpedo, as it's approaching. It's almost comic, in a way. You see it in the water and everything's suspended. You think, oh I see, here it comes.
(*He looks at her a moment.*)
It changes you. Before the war . . .
(*He smiles.*)
I was brought up, I was trained to be brilliant. Like the rest of my family. I played cricket, I would have a proper career. Running the country. It was simple, I was English. I thought the real world was real.
(JANETTA *frowns.*)
JANETTA: What do you mean? You haven't lost your ambition?
LEONARD: No. But it's different.
JANETTA: It sounds like you're saying all your will has gone.
(*He thinks a moment.*)

LEONARD: There's a smell. It's in the darkness. It's burning
   paintwork. And burning flesh. Then ether.
(*He is thoughtful, not looking at her.*)
JANETTA: You don't talk about it much.
LEONARD: No. That's what poetry's for. To say what can't be
   said.[29]

At the approach of the torpedo a moment stretches into infinity
until, as Leonard puts it, everything is suspended. The vision of
sudden death pulls him beyond temporality into a spot of time that
has lost none of its intense colour: 'It's burning paintwork. And
burning flesh.' If that experience has drained him of worldly
ambition, it has not, as Janetta suggests, destroyed his will. On the
contrary, it has revealed to him a world more 'real' than that around
him, permitting him to engage in a project requiring immense
strength – that of casting his emotions in words. By the same token,
his material poverty belies the wealth of his inner life. He is a true
romantic, one with whom Janetta is, for the moment, content.

But the torpedo may be read also as an ominous indicator of the
future. Leonard seems presciently aware of Ian, a corrupt landlord
with whom Janetta subsequently has an affair. Ian's attraction lies in
his possession of those things Leonard lacks. He seduces her by
giving her a watch and taking her to his club. When he convinces
her to stay with him he makes the same appeal to reality as does
Lambert Le Roux in *Pravda*:

You can waste your life sitting there with your poet. I've met these
kind of people. 'Oh, I think this; oh, I think that . . .' (*He spreads his
arms, dramatizing.*) 'Oh, I feel; oh, I don't feel . . .' Of course it's
fine. It's a great game. Especially for two players. (*He is suddenly
serious.*) But don't ever kid yourself it's anything else.
(*IAN suddenly seems almost angry.*)
You're lucky, you're privileged. Spend your life asking, 'What do
I *feel* about this? Do I *feel* I'm doing the right thing . . .' (*He pauses.*)
Or else you can just do it. I know which kind of person I like.[30]

Ian inhabits a nightmare in which the only thing of significance is
the circulation of matter. Typically, he sleeps with Janetta and then
sends her out collecting rent from his run-down properties. At the
same time, his compulsive recourse to the word 'feel' indicates a

lurking anxiety, as if he and even she are aware of a false note. Her acquiescence in Ian's contempt for emotional truth indicates a failure to engage fully with Leonard, a failure borne out by her lightly vulgarised defence of him: 'He wants to express what he saw in the war', she tells Ian.[31] Worse still, there is an implied contempt in her assumption that because Leonard does not speak of it, he is ignorant of her affair.

In fact the dramatic focus of *Heading Home* is Leonard's grief, a grief all the more intense for its concealment. 'What excuse shall I give?', Janetta asks, 'let's say . . . I lacked experience. I wanted to be out in the world, see people, get close to real life.'[32] If Leonard sees the torpedo as it nears him, Janetta deliberately turns away. As Beryl tells her, 'Staying innocent is just a kind of cowardice. . . . If you'd looked once . . . If you'd looked at Leonard, I mean really looked, looked deep, you'd have understood.'[33] Janetta uses innocence as a moral blindfold that allows her to overlook the pain she causes.

Self-deception of this order reveals a callousness on her part and is unexpectedly lasting in its results. Years later, Janetta admits that 'I understand to this day that people like Leonard do not speak their feelings. But I still to this day am not wholly sure why.'[34] She remains excluded forever from the workings of the human spirit. In the play's final moments she admits that 'These events, I suppose, detain me and me only. No one else remembers them, or if they do, then quite differently. To them, they yield a different meaning. I remember them as if they were yesterday. But of course I shall not remember them for long.'[35] Janetta has no Lazar, and is denied the possibility of re-enacting even a fragment of her past. As if that was not bad enough, she acknowledges that what survives in the memory – the ability to retrieve the past imaginatively – is subject to the corruption of time. No attempt is made to assert its permanence, and there is no suggestion of defiance: 'I remember them as if they were yesterday. But of course I shall not remember them for long.' The coldness of the comfort granted Janetta reflects her culpability in the events she recalls, for the lesson of *Heading Home* is that we compromise our deepest feelings at our peril. To overlook injustice and cruelty is only to condone it, and that is an indulgence we can ill afford. Once lost, innocence cannot be reclaimed.

Beryl's protectiveness of Leonard is representative of Hare's response to Thatcherism, consolidated in *The Secret Rapture* (1988), *Paris by Night* (1988), and his trilogy of plays, *Racing Demon* (1990), *Mumuring Judges* (1991) and *The Absence of War* (1993). Hare's

Thatcherites condemn themselves. Having humiliated a pressure group opposed to the dumping of nuclear waste, Marion, the Conservative Cabinet minister in *The Secret Rapture*, boasts: 'You blast them right out of the water. Hey, at this moment I could take them all on. The gloves are off. That's what's great. That's what's exciting. It's a new age. Fight to the death.'[36] Later on she defends herself with the remark: 'I've nothing on my conscience. I don't feel anything.'[37]

Her complacent self-regard is shared by Clara, the Conservative Euro MP in *Paris by Night*:

> A lot of us now are tired with all the old excuses. Just get on with things. There's been far too much living off the state. People get soft. They always think there's someone who'll solve their problems for them. I hate that softness.[38]

Pestered by an old business associate for money to help his crippled daughter, Clara responds by murdering him, and when her own son falls badly ill, she does not bother even to visit him in hospital. The only effective resistance she encounters is that of her husband Gerald, who confronts her with the words: 'You think you can get away with anything. No regard at all for anyone's feelings but your own. You're trash. You're just trash. You're human trash. And trash belongs in the dustbin.'[39] Fresh from Dennis Potter's *The Singing Detective*, Michael Gambon as Gerald points his gun at her and fires five times. As the script indicates, 'Blood and bones against the wall. She reels like a puppet with each shot.'[40] Given Clara's amorality it is fitting that the scene alludes to the pulps of Ross Macdonald and Jim Thompson. But as a former reviewer of crime novels[41] Hare knows the genre to be rooted in fantasy. Clara's satisfyingly sticky end belies the political reality the drama as a whole is meant to reflect; after all, Dennis Thatcher did not kill his wife when she waged war on the miners, and those of her chickens that have come home to roost have inconvenienced only her successors.

The Secret Rapture partakes of a similar optimism. Marion's part in the ruin of her sister, Isobel, springs from the same hard-boiled callousness advocated by Clara. Moreover, Isobel confirms the suspicion that Hare derives his concept of tragedy from *King Lear*. Like Cordelia she is vulnerable because of her honesty: 'What's the point of lying?' she asks Marion, 'Anyway it's wrong.'[42] Like Cordelia, Isobel pursues her ideals at the cost of her own interests:

'The great thing is to love', she says, 'If you're loved back then it's a bonus.'[43] Isobel's quiet, heroic faith in human nature shames the coarse piety of Marion's husband Tom, who claims 'to do business the way Jesus would have done it'.[44]

But, as in *Lear*, those who follow their hearts in an unjust world are doomed. Isobel is exploited without mercy, blackmailed into looking after their dead father's malicious girlfriend Katherine, and tricked into giving Marion control of her business. Even her personal life is manipulated. For business reasons Marion finds it expedient to encourage one of Isobel's colleagues, Irwin, in his pursuit of her. When Isobel rejects him, he shoots her dead.

The play's emotional impact arises not just out of her death; it is wrapped up in Hare's conviction that spiritual perfection is unacceptable to a fallen world – so much so that we have evolved an almost systemic reaction against it. As Marion tells Isobel, 'You spoil everything you touch. Everywhere you go, there are arguments. God, how I hate all this human stuff. Wherever you go, you cause misery. People crying, people not talking. It overwhelms me. Because you can't just live. Why can't you *live*, like other people?'[45] That this speech is delivered by Marion does not allow us to dismiss it, especially since it echoes criticism of Susan in *Plenty* and Raymond in *Strapless*, both of whom are, for all their virtues, morally culpable. Marion restates her case in the final scene, just before Isobel's funeral:

It's frightened me, ever since I was a child. My memory of childhood is of watching and always pretending. I don't have the right equipment. I can't interpret what people feel. I've stood at the side. Just watching. It's made me angry. I've been angry all my life. Because people's passions seem so out of control. (*She shakes her head slightly.*) You either say, 'Right, OK, I don't understand anything, I'll take some simple point of view, just in the hope of getting things done. Just achieve something, by pretending things are simpler than they are.' Or else you say, 'I will try to understand everything.' (*She smiles.*) Then I think you go mad.[46]

At which point, remarkably, Marion and her husband Tom begin to make love in the living room of Isobel's house. A murderer in all but deed, Marion is rehabilitated by self-awareness. She confesses her failure to empathise, and accepts that those cursed with a sense of justice are not properly of this world, that for them death is liberation. Her lovemaking with Tom only emphasises the intuition that Isobel's death is a deliverance to be celebrated rather than mourned.

If it comes off in production the scene ought to be a *coup de théâtre* justifying the play's title, as Hare explains: 'In Catholic theology, the "secret rapture" is the moment when the nun will become the bride of Christ: so it means death, or love of death, or death under life.'[47] In a theatrical context this recollects the insights of Shakespearean tragedy. At Lear's death, Edgar tells Kent to 'Look up, my lord',[48] as the royal spirit flutters beyond the void of Shakespeare's 'wooden O'. But what establishes Shakespeare's mastery of theatrical form is Kent's immediate denial:

> Vex not his ghost. O, let him pass, he hates him
> That would upon the rack of this tough world
> Stretch him out longer.[49]

No one is better prepared for death than those wedded to their ideals; this 'tough world' can only torture Lear's renewed and heightened sense of justice. The refusal to mourn takes us to the heart of tragedy; as Lady Gregory put it, 'Tragedy must be a joy to the man who dies.'[50] Writing of Lear and Hamlet, Yeats observed that

> they, should the last scene be there,
> The great stage curtain about to drop,
> If worthy their prominent part in the play,
> Do not break up their lines to weep.
> They know that Hamlet and Lear are gay;
> Gaiety transfiguring all that dread.[51]

In Howard Davies' National Theatre production of *The Secret Rapture* Isobel's ghost passed across the back of the stage in the final moments, though no such action is indicated in the published text. Leaving aside its awkwardness in an otherwise naturalistic play, its desired effect – that of emotional release – undermines the play's tragic purpose by appealing to sentiment. In the play as written, in which Marion's final question goes unanswered – 'Isobel, where are you? (*She waits a moment.*) Isobel, why don't you come home?'[52] – the secret rapture, the very knub of tragedy, is fully realised. And in any case, Hare offers solace enough without the resurrection of its heroine. Marion's reformed humanism, indicated by her love-making in her sister's living room, provides a curiously heartened resolution to the play's political subtext. Its confident advocacy of liberal values is what makes *The Secret Rapture* less rueful about Thatcherism than one might expect.

No other work pinpoints Hare's concerns as a dramatic writer more accurately than the trilogy of plays composed between 1987 and 1993. By any standards it is a remarkable achievement, one of the few genuinely epic works by a contemporary playwright. It sets out to examine the changes that have occurred in British society as mediated through three institutions, all of which reached crisis point during the 1980s: the Church, the Law and the Labour Party. Hare's choice of subject arose partly from his conviction that 'British society needs not to abolish its institutions, but to refresh them. For, if not through institutions, how do we express the common good?'[53] The trilogy is impelled both by a deep belief in the common good and by a profound sense of moral outrage at the damage done to it by Thatcherite policies. And lest there were doubts about Hare's connectedness with the outside world, it draws on a great deal of research in the field. A selection of this material has been published as *Asking Around: Background to the David Hare Trilogy* (1993), the introduction to which provides an excellent preface to the trilogy as a whole.

Racing Demon and *Murmuring Judges* argue that, when they are compelled to submit to the rules of the market-place, neither the law nor the clergy can live up to the principles of fairness and justice on which they are supposedly founded. In *Racing Demon* the evangelical wing of the church has turned to a form of showbusiness to attract congregations; the Bishop of Southwark tells the doubting clergyman, Lionel, who is the play's protagonist, that 'As a priest you have only one duty. That's to put on a show.'[54] But if Hare finds the evangelical movement symptomatic of Thatcherism, he refuses to condemn it outright. Its strongest advocate is Lionel's young colleague, Tony:

> Educated clerics don't like evangelicals, because evangelicals drink sweet sherry and keep budgerigars and have ducks in formations on their walls. (*Nods, smiling.*) Yes, and they also have the distressing downmarket habit of trying to get people emotionally involved. (*Stares at them.*) You know I'm right. And – as it happens – I went to a grammar school, I was brought up –

unlike you – among all those normal, decent people who shop at Allied Carpets and are into DIY. And I don't think they should always be looked down on.[55]

Institutional elitism is identified from an early point in Hare's writing as part of the 'moral gumrot'[56] of British society. There could be no clearer admission of the contempt it implies than that of Sir Peter Edgecombe QC in *Murmuring Judges*, as he remonstrates with his young counsel, Irina Platt: 'Think about it, Irina. It's not such a terrible thing. I hate to have to tell you, it'll come as a shock to you, but, by definition, sub-average is what nearly 50 per cent of the entire population is fated to be.'[57] Fate has nothing to do with it, except as a divine sanction by which this grim fiction may be transformed into fact. Sir Peter is the spokesman for a profession that guards its interests by means of exclusion, like any other club. He argues that very point in ridiculing Irina's wish to reform the police: 'You simply cannot be this naïve. It's called a force. Police *force*, that's the name for it. Everyone knows. It's the wrong word. If I could pass an Act of Parliament, I'd call it what it actually is. (*He smiles.*) "Club." Police club. And unless you can find someone who's interested in jacking in their membership, you haven't got a cat's chance in hell.'[58]

According to Tony in *Racing Demon*, evangelism threatens the church by its 'distressing downmarket habit of trying to get people emotionally involved', taking us in a single phrase to the point at which politics and ethics meet. Like Brenton, Hare regards alienation as a form of derangement. In *Wetherby* Morgan is literally crazed by emotional deprivation: 'I want some feeling!', he screams, 'I want some contact!' And one of the characters in *The Secret Rapture* is 'so out of touch with his feelings that he's like some great half-dead animal that lies there, just thrashing about'.[59] *Racing Demon* and *Murmuring Judges* explain repression as a function of politics. 'It seems so obvious to an outsider', Irina tells Sir Peter. 'Do you not really know? All this behaviour, the honours, the huge sums of money, the buildings, the absurd dressing-up. They do have a purpose. It's anaesthetic. It's to render you incapable of imagining life the other way round.'[60] The exertion of power demands that we suspend our sympathy in the name of our own innate superiority. This is of course one of those insights vouchsafed to Lear: 'Thorough tatter'd clothes [small] vices do appear;/ Robes and furr'd gowns hide all.'[61] As Lear is to discover, such wisdom serves only to further mock our sense of justice. In tragedy, wisdom is just an added source of torment.

But unlike *The Secret Rapture*, neither *Racing Demon* nor *Murmuring Judges* is finally tragic. Between the innate conservativism of the institution and the extremity of those wishing to reform it, Hare charts a course towards the depths of romantic possibility. Siding neither with Lionel, who is 'Caught in a cycle of decline',[62] nor with Tony, who is seduced by 'The illusion of action',[63] *Racing Demon* instead centres on values that have always inspired Hare. Addressing God, the Rev. Donald 'Streaky' Bacon, another of Tony's colleagues, admits that

> I have no theology. Can't do it. By my bed, there's a pile of paperbacks called *The Meaning of Meaning*, and *How to Ask Why*. They've been there for years. The whole thing's so clear. You're there. In people's happiness. Tonight, in the taste of that drink. Or the love of my friends. The whole thing's so simple. Infinitely loving.
>   Why do people find it so hard?[64]

Streaky has no need of theology because his sense of the divine is interfused with experience of everyday pleasures. His tacit assumption of our irretrievably fallen nature short circuits the need for a moral purism designed to reclaim paradise. The garden of heavenly delights surrounds us on earth: as the Koran puts it, 'Allah is as close as the vein in your neck.' In 1988 Hare told Vera Lustig that 'Nobody seems to have spotted it, but I've found myself in *Wetherby*, in *Paris by Night*, in *The Secret Rapture*, and in *Strapless* drawn more and more to feeling that there's something which isn't just what we're conditioned by. . . . If a writer doesn't have a sense of the other, by which I mean spirit or soul, I don't want to know.'[65] Such intimations promise a milder day of which Hare is, unfashionably, one of the few prophets in contemporary theatre. Thus *Murmuring Judges* concludes with proposals of legal reform, and *Racing Demon* with sublimity:

> I love that bit when the plane begins to climb, the ground smooths away behind you, the buildings, the hills. Then the white patches. The vision gets bleary. The cloud becomes a hard shelf. The land is still there. But all you see is white and the horizon.
>   And then you turn and head towards the sun.[66]

The third play in the trilogy, *The Absence of War*, necessarily steps
back from that kind of optimism, as its subject is a dark moment in
history – the general election of 1992 as experienced by the Labour
Party. Like some of Hare's other protagonists, George Jones, the
fictionalised Party leader, embodies aspects of the tragic hero. While
discussing with Oliver Dix, his political adviser, whether Labour
can win the election, he even alludes to the Shakespearean model:

> GEORGE: (*Smiles*) Go to the theatre, I keep telling you. Brutus
> has qualms.
> OLIVER: What does that mean?
> GEORGE: There's a scene in a tent. Before battle. All leaders
> have them. In plays, the leader always has a quiet crisis.
> OLIVER: Then? Then what happens?
> GEORGE: Oh then . . .
> (*He smiles, deliberately playful.*)
> OLIVER: Come on, tell me. I didn't read English.
> (GEORGE *stirs now, thoughtful.*)
> GEORGE: It's all right, Oliver. Then they always murder their
> doubts.
> OLIVER: Thank God for that.[67]

At which point, in performance, the audience has a laugh at Oliver's
expense. After all, he has failed to understand George's allusion,
and remains unaware of Brutus' defeat, his encounter with Caesar's
ghost, or his part in Caesar's murder. But if the joke appears to be on
Oliver, it only compounds the irony that George embodies aspects
of both Caesar and his trusted colleague: like Brutus, he is doomed
to lose the war; like Caesar, he will be betrayed by his friends.

I have already observed that the tragic hero in Hare's work is
essentially selfless: Isobel in *The Secret Rapture* loves others without
expecting any return; Lionel in *Racing Demon* sticks by a promise
which he gave in good faith even if it means the end of his career.
George refuses to listen to his colleagues when they warn him of the
political ambitions of his Shadow Chancellor, Malcolm Pryce,
preferring to think the best of him. He sacrifices his own standing
in order to support Malcolm even when it becomes clear that he has
leaked damaging information about the Party to the media.
Politically, George is a loser because he puts the good of the Party
– and of the country at large – before himself.

After the defeat, Oliver scolds him for giving his support to Malcolm, who is to succeed him as Party leader:

OLIVER: You call this strength? It's the most miserable weakness. (*He turns from across the ballroom.*) You will give him a loyalty he never gave you.

GEORGE: I have to. Yes. Because I believe in the Party. I'm not sentimental. The Party is not my whole life. But it's all we have. It's the only practical instrument that exists in this country for changing people's lives for the good.[68]

George behaves in a just manner not because he is isolated from the world, but because, like Lionel in *Racing Demon*, he is a pragmatist. He wants to better people's lives, and realises that the only way to do that is to carry a united Party into the election and beyond. This is what Oliver means when he observes that George 'likes to take one step back from things. . . . It's the bloody theatre. He likes tragedy too much. I don't. To me, tragedy's just a posh word for losing.'[69] A central insight of tragedy is that love transcends the world of politics, an insight gained only by standing back from the flux of human affairs and appreciating the larger forces at work in peoples' lives; as George puts it: 'Our master is justice.'[70] Such insights may be correct, but they have no bearing on the outcome of general elections.

George's most selfless act is his submission to the campaign strategy devised by Oliver. After a mistake in front of the cameras years before, he has surrounded himself with advisers who strictly monitor his words and actions. A new publicity agent, Lindsay, sees the problem more clearly than anyone else, and explains it to George's minder, Andrew:

LINDSAY: George once made a blunder, what was it, six years ago . . .?

ANDREW: Not one blunder, Lindsay.

LINDSAY: And for that you still want to punish him. You decided for some reason to smother his wit. All his gaiety. His humour.

(ANDREW *turns away, angry now.*)

ANDREW: Nonsense. That's nonsense.

LINDSAY: And that's why he's angry. Underneath George is always bloody furious. He's angry. And who can blame him?

(GEORGE *watches, giving nothing away.*)
　　Everything in him wants to let rip.
(ANDREW *looks to* GEORGE, *but* LINDSAY *goes straight on.*)
　　The public aren't stupid. They know he's been programmed.
　　It's not hard to work out why this man's ratings are low. The
　　public see only one thing when they look at him, and that's
　　six rolls of sticky tape wrapped around his mouth . . .[71]

Like *Plenty* and *Wetherby*, *The Absence of War* examines the
psychology of repression, but where Susan and Morgan defied it,
George surrenders himself to it. As Gwenda, his diary secretary
comments, 'There's one rule with George. Never slacken the
leash.'[72] And, significantly, Malcolm is the foremost of those who
demand that George's speeches be scripted rather than impro-
vised.[73] Lindsay correctly notes the destructive effects of this
strategy: by coming between him and the electorate, it destroys
both the Party's chances at the polls, as well as George's political
career. This is not empty theorising, a plot twist devised by the
author to spice up the drama; it is true to real events. In *Asking
Around*, Hare transcribes a conversation in which Jack Cunningham
persuaded Neil Kinnock not to crack any jokes about the
Conservatives. 'Cool, cool. Play it safe', Cunningham advises.
'You're telling *me* to play it safe? You're telling *me* to play it
safe?', Kinnock responds, 'I'm the only man wearing a bloody corset
over his mouth.'[74]
　　As Lindsay observes, the strategy derives from a lack of
confidence that has led the Party to fight the election on grounds
dictated by their enemies: 'Keep George in a box. And meanwhile
try to out-Tory the Tories. . . . And by this appalling coincidence, it
also robs George of what he does best . . . (*She nods.*) George became
Leader because of a quality he had. That quality came from his
passion.'[75] Having suppressed his rage at social injustice, along with
his essential appeal to the electorate, George changes course during
the last week of the campaign, and tries to rediscover his ability to
speak directly to the people. But he fails. Delivering a speech at a
rally in Manchester, he dries up when he attempts to depart from
the script written by his advisers. Afterwards he reflects:

All those hours in hotel rooms working at speeches, drafting, re-
drafting, polishing, changing every word and all you're doing is

covering up for what's really gone wrong. What you know in your heart. What really happened. What *really* happened . . .
(*He pauses a moment. The others are suddenly still in the middle of his stream of consciousness.*)
You once had the words. Now you don't.[76]

The full impact of his failure is felt only when he perceives the extent of his alienation from his own feelings. In this sense at least, he is truly a representative of the people. After all, his Party has followed the same course. Vera Klein, a Labour activist in her seventies, recalls how, 40 years ago, 'we thrived on discussion. To disagree meant you were alive. Now it's taken as a sign of disloyalty. What is this fear we have of it now?'[77] These points extend a discussion which began in *Wetherby*, when Morgan praised 'good old words' like revenge and anger on the grounds that they spoke directly to the emotions. 'If you can't feel them', he told Roger, 'you might as well be dead.'[78] Feeling is what brings people together; it affirms them as individuals and as groups – and gives them power. By voting against George, the electorate reject the innate moral sense that might have revealed to them his virtues; in doing so, they reject the only candidate with their interests at heart. This echoes Neil Kinnock in *Asking Around*, when Hare asks him whether, after the election, he doesn't feel let down by the voters.

> KINNOCK: The people let themselves down. They went into the polling booth and voted to stab their own grandparents and children in the chest. But I don't hate them for it. You'd go mad if you hated the public.[79]

Kinnock's forbearance is shared by George. When Oliver points out that 'the people do stupid things. Like wear your bloody T-shirt and then vote against you', George replies that 'It's their right. It's the only right they've got.'[80] The silence that follows that speech – both in print and in performance – indicates the strength of feeling behind it. Nor is it possible to disentangle this aspect of George's character from Hare's own feelings. Attending a Labour Party rally in Sheffield, he notes that 'For thirteen years people have been waiting patiently, effectively dispossessed, their values laughed at and their interests unrepresented. Now at last they are ready, on the brink of having a voice again.'[81] That deep sympathy for those alienated by Thatcherism informs this play and the trilogy of which it is the concluding part.

The Absence of War may look back to *Julius Caesar* in its handling of doubt and betrayal, but George is neither Caesar nor Brutus. His values are more like those of a religious leader than of a politician. In fact, at a celebratory meeting with his advisers, he behaves very much like Christ at the Last Supper: 'GEORGE *takes the chair at the head of the table. Then he takes the hands of* MARY *and* OLIVER *beside him and holds them a moment affectionately. Then he starts to eat.*'[82] Like Jesus, George has the ability to bring people together in harmony – and at one point he even declares that this is his function, comparing himself with Bunyan's hero. When Lindsay asks him how it feels to be constrained by his advisers, he replies:

> Lindsay, for goodness sake, this is my burden. Like Pilgrim, this is the course I am on. (*He is suddenly firm.*) You can never let go. You can never lose sight of the problem that when this Party fell into my hands, it was torn, disfigured, unelectable. With a matchless capacity for meaningless squabbles and fights. So changing that culture, changing that disastrous habit of anarchy, controlling the Party, getting it to speak with one voice, this has been my historical legacy.[83]

If *The Absence of War* has its tragic side, like the other works in the trilogy, it refuses to submit to despair. George may lose the election, but over the long term his 'historical legacy' is assured – the Party will survive. He understands, probably from reading Shakespeare, that political leaders come and go, but the Party, the only 'practical instrument' for change, has to be preserved. At the beginning of the campaign, George and his colleagues drink a toast. 'To Pilgrim', Lindsay says, 'May he win through!'[84] What saves the play from tragedy is that he does.

7

Alan Ayckbourn: Beyond Romanticism

'All I'm saying is – isn't it ironic that the hero is forgotten? And the villain has now become the hero. That's all. And isn't that a reflection of our time?'[1] 'All I'm saying', 'That's all': the verbal tics that punctuate the question posed by the television reporter in Alan Ayckbourn's *Man of the Moment*, suggest that by 1988 it was too obvious to be worth asking. They serve also to camouflage the implied political critique; after all, complicity is the theme also of Hare's *Heading Home* and Brenton's *Berlin Bertie*. Odd company, perhaps, for the 'non-political Priestley'[2] of British theatre to be keeping, but Ayckbourn sides with Brenton and Hare in regarding the betrayal of personal ethics as analogous to political corruption. Like theirs, his political consciousness dates back to the 1950s when, as they would agree, this country fell from grace. 'At one stage', Ayckbourn recalls,

> there was this terrible old patriarchal society where Mr Macmillan was obviously the most honest man in the world; he'd shot a few grouse and things but knew what was good for you. He was like some sort of old uncle, really. And then somebody discovered that there was as much corruption in politics as in the rest of the world. One wasn't so surprised by that, because politicians are representatives of us – we voted them in. But then *everything* became corrupt! I mean everything. We didn't believe in anything.[3]

Ayckbourn is critical less of the duplicity revealed by such events as the Suez crisis than of the deeper malaise of which it was symptomatic. This preoccupation takes dramatic shape in *Man of the Moment*. Despite being a convicted criminal, having robbed a bank and blasted a shotgun into a woman's face, Vic Parks now resides in a Mediterranean villa on the spoils of his success as a

television personality. His saleability in the British media depends
on a hypocritical repudiation of his former life. As his wife Trudy
tells the man who foiled the robbery 17 years before: 'I wasn't
around when – when all that happened – I mean, Vic and I, we've
only been married eight years. . . . By the time I met Vic that was all
in the past. I wasn't a part of it and I don't really want to know about
it. We're all different people now.'[4] But Trudy's disavowals are too
fretted, and her reading of human psychology too simplistic, to be
taken at face value. Confronted by a witness to her husband's
criminal past, she abandons her natural defensiveness and accepts
that 'I'm a part of Vic. I married him, knowing what he'd done to
another human being. To another woman. And I had his children
knowing that. I took on all of him. What do they say these days?
(*Smiling faintly.*) A wife should be responsible for her husband's
debts.'[5] By accepting her accountability Trudy takes the most
important moral journey in the play.

If, as Ayckbourn suggests, *Man of the Moment* depicts 'a direct
confrontation between good and evil',[6] its concept of wickedness
allows little room for Trudy's denials. Douglas Beechey (the man
who foiled the robbery) is now married to Nerys, into whose face
Vic shot his gun. When Vic asks the reason for his visit, Douglas
replies that

> you're still there. In our dreams, you see. After seventeen years.
> We still both dream about you. We wake up occasionally. In the
> night. Nerys has this terrible fear – it's quite ridiculous, I've told
> her – that one night you're going to break in downstairs and come
> up to get her. I've said to her, it's ridiculous – I mean, there you
> are on the telly twice a week or something, helping the kids or
> telling the old folk to mind how they go – I said, he's not going to
> want to break in here, Nerys – Not after seventeen years, is he?
> Still. You can't always control your imagination, can you? No
> matter how hard you try. So, don't take this wrong, but I was
> hoping this – meeting – might help to exorcise you. If you follow
> me. I told you it would sound peculiar.[7]

Amused rather than offended, Vic fails to see that Nerys remains
undeceived by his adopted role as guardian of public safety, bound
forever to her apprehension of him at the moment he shot her in the
face. She identifies him – correctly, as it turns out – as a malign
spirit. But the play's hardest lesson is that such forces defy exorcism.

Like Trudy, we remain in some sense wedded to evil, and mere recognition is not sufficient to disempower it.

Against these bleak misgivings the best Ayckbourn can offer is Douglas, described by Jill, the television producer who arranges his reunion with Vic, as having a 'dreary flock-wallpaper personality'.[8] When she asks him whether he feels strongly about anything, he replies:

DOUGLAS: (*Thoughtfully*) I suppose evil, really.
JILL: Evil?
DOUGLAS: Yes. I feel strongly about that.
JILL: That's it? Just evil?
DOUGLAS: Yes. Only, it's often hard to recognize. But there's a lot of it about, you know.[9]

The comic banality of Douglas' language indicates a lack of ambition reflected in his career as a double-glazing salesman and residence in a 'damp little house' on a main road. A fool he may be, but he is redeemed by an unhesitating moral sense. When he tells Trudy about how he thwarted the bank robbery, he confesses that 'I don't know why I did what I did. Your husband was right, it was madness. It just seemed the only thing to do at the time, that's all.'[10] An otherwise unremarkable man, Douglas pulled off a feat of extraordinary courage through an *unthinking* response; we intellectualise our reactions only at the risk of losing touch with them. At the same time, Douglas is firmly located in a world in which villainy always has the upper hand. By his own account his heroism was 'madness' – inviting comparison with Shakespeare's 'foolish' protagonist, Lear. Lear's belief in the immortality of his relationship with Cordelia may be unshakeable, but that can't prevent her death. And, since the opinions and uses of this world are no better disposed to Douglas' heroism than to Lear's love of his daughter, the real men of the moment will always be the villains.

This essentially tragic view of human nature reaches back at least to *A Chorus of Disapproval* (1984). Like *Man of the Moment*, it is set in a world in which corruption is taken for granted. When Jarvis Huntley-Pike, the local squire, interferes with The Pendon Amateur Light Operatic Society's production of *The Beggar's Opera*, its director, Dafydd, calls him an 'interfering old fascist'.[11] Dafydd later refers to him as 'Councillor Huntley-Potty-Pike. One of the whizz kids on our Council. Which explains why this town's in the state it is.'[12] This is a sound judgement and, as political comment, *A Chorus of Disapproval* is an unexpectedly important play. The critique of Huntley-Pike extends over generations. At one point Jarvis discusses a piece of land in the village which was bought by his grandfather, Joshua, and given to the village as a cricket pitch:

> Only one thing – bearing in mind he were a chapel man – not on Sundays, lads. Never on the sabbath. Well, any road up, year or so later, he's out for a stroll one Sunday afternoon with his children and grandchildren – taking the air, like – and what should he spy as he's passing the cricket field but a bunch of workers laughing and joking and chucking a ball about like it were Saturday dinner time. And the old man says nowt. Not at the time. But the next day, Monday morning first thing, he sends in his bulldozers and diggers and ploughs and he digs that land up from one end to the other. Then he sets fire to t'pavilion and he puts up a 12-foot wooden fence. Palings. And to this day, not a ball has been thrown on that field. That's the sort of man he was. Me grandfather. Dying breed.[13]

Jarvis recounts this tale as if it were to his credit, unaware that it amounts to a indictment of the ruthlessness and mean-spiritedness that once characterised the squirearchy. He is implicated in his grandfather's high-handed behaviour, not just because he was present at the time, but because he continues to prevent the land from being used. That meanness permeates the community – down even to the landlord of the local pub, who has ice but won't give it to his customers. As Dafydd observes: 'You can't charge for it, don't put it out. That's his maxim. His beer mats are screwed to the bar.'[14] All of which makes Pendon a good home for BLM, a multi-national company that produces vast profits, but ploughs none back into the community on which it depends.

Most of the audience with whom I saw the play at the National Theatre in 1986 found such observations slightly too close to the bone for outright hilarity. They provide the faintest outline of a country in painful transition from the paternalistic conservativism of Mr Macmillan to Mrs Thatcher's enterprise culture. Into its midst Ayckbourn drops the licensed roguery of *The Beggar's Opera*, with its pimps, whores and highwaymen. If Gay's characters seem more innocent than those of Pendon it is probably because their vices go unconcealed; as Dafydd tells the new recruit to his production, Guy:

DAFYDD: I'm absolutely convinced that this show – first produced when was it – ? 1728 – it's as entertaining and as vital and as relevant as it was then . . . Suky Tawdry . . . Dolly Trull . . . Mrs Vixen . . . Those are the whores and pimps of the town . . . almost see their faces in their names, can't you? Polly Peachum. That tells you all you need to know about her, doesn't it? What an age, eh? What an age. Well, compared to our own.

GUY: Yes. Yes. Of course, they didn't have any . . .

DAFYDD: I mean, look at us today. Sex shops, I ask you. Can you imagine Captain Macheath furtively purchasing marital aids . . . ? What's happening to us, Guy? What's happening to us, eh?[15]

The inspired conceit of Captain Macheath furtively purchasing marital aids takes us to the ethical core of the play. For the world of the mid-1980s, as represented by Pendon, is too full of deceit and disguise to sustain the mutual trust enjoyed by Gay's characters; as Dafydd recognises, it is the covert nature of evil in the modern world that separates us from them. Appearance is no longer a dependable guide to character, for as Lear remarks, 'a dog's obey'd in office. . . . Robes and furr'd gowns hide all.'[16] This has always been a rich seam in literature; Webster and Tourneur mined it by making the villain their hero, taking as protagonists the inside dealers of their time, upwardly mobile young Machiavels who stabbed and poisoned their way to the grave. Ayckbourn instead hands the stage to the most unlikely of protagonists – Dafydd, an unhappily-married, small-time solicitor who stages an amateur production of *The Beggar's Opera* to admonish his fellow citizens; 'in the real world out there', as he admits, 'I actually am in serious trouble and I couldn't give a stuff.'[17]

If Dafydd's enterprise is as futile as Lear's carving-up of his kingdom, the revival of Gay's long-forgotten entertainment nevertheless reminds us of a cultural birthright from which we have been disinherited, a tradition of writing in which we observe the world not as it is, but as it might be. Only against the landlord's wishes do the cast burst into a spontaneous rendition of one of Gay's songs: 'Fill ev'ry Glass, for Wine inspires us,/ And fires us/ With Courage, Love and Joy.' 'Marvellous music, isn't it?' Dafydd says to Guy, 'All traditional tunes, you know. All the tunes Gay used were traditional.'[18] But by 1986 tradition was long out of fashion, and wish-fulfilment was the refuge of the dispossessed. When the actor playing Macheath resigns from the production, Dafydd himself admits that

> nobody really cares. Not in this country. Anything you want to mention's more important than theatre to most of them. Washing their hair, cleaning their cars ... If this was Bulgaria or somewhere we'd have peasants hammering on the doors. Demanding satisfaction or their money back. This place, you tell them you're interested in the arts, you get messages of sympathy. Get well soon.[19]

Ayckbourn is no ideologue, but Dafydd's remarks confirm his commitment to the immaterial. If we find the Bulgarian peasants no more substantial than Gay's characters, they still provide a model for the potential investment – moral, imaginative, political – to be made in theatre. In any case, the example of Czechoslovakia, where a revolution born in a theatre swept a playwright to power, lends credibility to the 'peasants hammering on the doors', though, as Seamus Heaney has suggested, such miracles occur but 'once in a lifetime'.[20]

Dafydd's displacement is all the more poignant in extending beyond physical barriers, for his rightful home is Gay's guileless world. 'I trust you',[21] he tells Guy, leaving him to guard his pint at the bar, which is readily consumed in his absence. Dafydd's failure correctly to interpret this slip betrays his instincts. 'This casting business', he remarks, 'I have a feeling, an instinctive feeling in my bones, you know, and I'm not often wrong – sometimes, not often – that you'd make a pretty good Crook-Finger'd Jack.'[22] Ayckbourn's focus on character is so sharp, and the ironies so lightly registered, that this remark makes its impact only in retrospect. Dafydd can be aware neither that a combination of luck and corruption will promote Guy, ultimately, to the starring role of Macheath, nor that the 'instinctive feeling' that he is a 'pretty good Crook-Finger'd Jack' is truer to Guy's character than he supposes.

A king in the rehearsal room, Dafydd is less prosperous in real life. His name for Guy, 'My rock',[23] carries the same ironic connotations as in the Bible, where it is given to the most faithful of the disciples, by whom Christ is denied. Similarly, Dafydd places his trust in a man who proceeds to have an affair with his wife. Guy betrays Dafydd a second time by cheating him on a deal to buy Huntley-Pike's plot of land. Like Douglas Beechey, also played by Michael Gambon, Dafydd is a holy fool whose good nature is an invitation to the unscrupulous. As Ayckbourn says: 'It's my theory that if a man of the stature of Jesus Christ came back now we'd all be trying to figure his angle. . . . Because in a world of dishonest people could we recognize an honest man?'[24]

Such intimations of moral confusion imply tragedy, though it doesn't necessarily follow; after all, Claudio's denunciation of Hero does not lead to her death. As it happens, both *Much Ado About Nothing* and *A Chorus of Disapproval* evade tragic dénouements by allowing romantic possibilities to intervene. This updated variation on the *Deus ex machina* is managed in the former by Benedick and Beatrice and in the latter by Gay's Player, who interrupts the action to inform us that 'The Catastrophe is manifestly wrong, for an Opera must end happily. All this we must do to comply with the Taste of the Town.'[25] Since Ayckbourn is too scrupulous a technician to allow such liberties to pass unexplained, and too honest not to acknowledge the opportunism of playing to the audience, his stage directions confess that, 'as with *The Beggar's Opera* itself, the performance ends happily and triumphantly (if a trifle cynically).'[26]

The admission of cynicism allows Ayckbourn to have a happy ending while denying responsibility for it. All the same, it suggests an unease about the idealising tendency, and in subsequent works he has found ingenious ways of continuing his flirtation with it at a safe distance. The fantasy life conducted by Susan, the heroine of *Woman in Mind* (1985), provides the colour missing from her drab life as the spouse of a clergyman: leisure, happy families, sunshine. Her imaginary husband, Andy, even provides her with love:

we'd all be lost without you. There's only one of you, you see. (*Smiling slightly*) Unfortunately. And we all need you very much. Me most especially. I mean, after all, what does Tony stand to lose? Just a big sister. So what? Plenty of those. Ten a penny. And Lucy? Well – girls and their mothers. We all know what they're like. She'd soon get over it. But me? I'd be losing a wife. And that I'd never get over. Not one as dear and as precious as you. (*He kisses her tenderly.*)
Whom, incidentally, I love more than words can ever say . . .[27]

Andy's clichéd, platitudinous delivery merely reflects the elements from which he has been constructed – the films Susan has seen[28] and the historical romances she has read,[29] her appetite for which is itself symptomatic of unfulfilled needs. As Ayckbourn notes, her dream world is 'Unashamedly romantic, very high gloss, way over the top, as if from some super soap opera, full of laughter and flashing teeth.'[30] But in spite of its manner, Andy's declaration should in performance be invested with all the tenderness and affection lacking in Susan's everyday existence, for it is that intensity that makes him, and what he represents, so compulsively appealing.

You don't need a degree in psychiatry to predict the consequences: as Susan's ideal world becomes more florid, her commitment to it increases. Ayckbourn is fond of the notion that comedies are 'tragedies that have been interrupted';[31] his refusal to intervene in Susan's favour typifies the tragic impulse behind his work during the 1980s. The play's humour is thus painfully compromised. For instance, Susan's imaginary daughter, Lucy, remarks that 'last Sunday in the *Observer*, they called you probably our most important living historical novelist',[32] and later asks: 'Do you know what it said in the *Sunday Times* about you, last week? It said you were the most brilliant woman heart surgeon there was in this country.'[33] Like Tony's declaration of love, these testimonials pander too extravagantly to Susan's emotions not to amuse us. But we laugh at our peril, for the effusions of her invisible friends bear witness to a steadily diminishing sense of worth. Never will Susan achieve any of the things for which they praise her, and she knows it. 'What are you hoping for, Muriel?' she asks her husband's sister. 'A phantom pregnancy? (*She laughs.*) Too late, dear. Too damn late. You and me both. Over the hill.'[34]

That pervasive sense of waste is what finally gives *Woman in Mind* its tragic shape, for Ayckbourn conceives of tragedy in structural terms rather than as moments when the affective energy of the drama precipitates in a single, appalling apprehension – as when Desdemona dies defending Othello.[35] That's not to say that Ayckbourn is any less concerned with content than Shakespeare; on the contrary, he has defined tragedy in distinctly moral terms: 'It is to do with choices we make, wrong choices, leading to further wrong choices.'[36] Jerome, the composer of the near future in *Henceforward . . .* (1987), is faced with the decision of whether or not to return to his wife and daughter from whom he was separated four years earlier. It should not be a difficult one, especially in view of the fact that he has been unable to compose since he last saw his daughter, Geain: 'I need her back more than anything in the world', he says.[37] But that emotional void has been filled, insidiously, by his machines. His only contact with other human beings is through the answerphone and closed circuit television mounted on his front door, and, as he admits, he hasn't spoken to anyone 'for months'.[38] Most tellingly of all, he cohabits with a female robot called Nan who, he says, 'has more dignity, more sense of loyalty and responsibility than any other fifty women you can name put together'.[39] Nothing could more clearly indicate the extent of his alienation; like that of Susan's dreams, the ideal world he has programmed to his specifications has more attraction than real human beings and their emotions. 'If human beings behaved a bit less like human beings and a bit more like machines, we'd all be better off',[40] he tells his wife.

With these remarks Ayckbourn's critique of idealism takes its most extreme form, allowing no doubt that the endless spiral of wish-fulfilment to which Susan and Jerome commit themselves is inhumane. As Corinna, Jerome's wife, explains to Geain: 'In the past, your father and I, we have – we have both been selfish, we have been thoughtless and stupid and – human. But we have also been, in our time, warm and spontaneous and amusing and joyful and – loving. Which is something we can also be, because we are human. But which that machine can never be.'[41] There are no models for real life; it can be neither replicated nor programmed. The hopes of idealists throughout history have failed because they believed they had discovered the behavioural blueprint for the millennium. Jerome's own utopian schemes depend on the belief that love can be logged onto a floppy disk:

I want to express the feeling of love in an abstract musical form. In such a way that anyone who hears it – *anyone* – no matter what language they speak – no matter what creed or colour – they will recognize it – and respond to it – and relate it to their own feelings of love that they have or they've experienced at some time – so they say – yes, my God, that's it! That's what it is! And maybe who knows, consequently, there might be a bit more of it.[42]

We may sympathise with his aspirations, but Jerome's model of social improvement is just as regimented and totalitarian as any other: 'no matter what language they speak . . . they *will* recognize it'. His 'abstract musical form' boils all the blips and hiccups of human thought down to a single level – unanswering, invariable, compliant. Ayckbourn has described it as 'pure subliminal advertising for the good life',[43] underlining its materialism, for in Jerome's view love is not merely formulaic, it's a marketable commodity of which he is the campaign manager.

Since, like all Ayckbourn's work, this play adheres to the rules of romance, Jerome is offered the second chance he would be denied in real life. 'You want me back with you?' he asks Corinna.

> CORINNA: Yes.
> JEROME: Why?
> CORINNA: (*Desperately, at the end of her tether*) Because we both love you, Jerome. God knows why, but we love you. Love, love, love! All right.[44]

This is the crucial intervention by which tragedy might become comedy; in this case it does not succeed. Unresponsive to the emotional appeal of his wife's words, Jerome prefers to remain at his synthesiser, sampling and re-recording the phrase 'Love, love, love!' until he produces his 'abstract musical form'. 'Anything you want to mention's more important than theatre to most of them. Washing their hair, cleaning their cars . . .' Dafydd's attack on the middle classes of 1980s Britain could apply equally well to Jerome, their descendant in the near future as Ayckbourn envisaged it in 1987. Like them, Jerome fails to distinguish between substance and shadow, between the things that affirm our common humanity, and those which isolate us. Ayckbourn recalls the first production of the play, and how 'I said to the actress playing it, "never should a woman have said 'I love you' with more conviction than this woman does, and never has a man been so loved with no holds barred, and never has he turned away a bigger bunch of flowers"'.[45] It is typical of Ayckbourn's disillusionment with the materialism of the late 1980s that he can write with such intensity about its essential inhumanity.

The implied political subtext surfaces in *A Small Family Business* (1987). Its protagonist, Jack McCracken, is a businessman who is 'unbelievably' honest.[46] He refers explicitly to the degraded ethics of the age when accepting his job as managing director:

Now it's very hard in this country for a business man to say something even halfway idealistic, without people falling over backwards laughing. To them it sounds like a contradiction in terms, anyway. But. Putting it as simply as I can. If I do nothing else, and during the coming months I can assure you I plan to do plenty, but if I succeed in doing nothing else I am determined to introduce one simple concept. And that concept is basic trust.[47]

Jack's 'simple concept' is too much for human nature; as his wife tells him, 'If the whole bloody world was as good as you there'd be no problem.'[48] But even those members of his own family involved in running the business cannot understand him,[49] and force him to abandon first one principle then another, until eventually he perpetrates several acts of bribery and a murder. Jack may start out with good intentions, but his corruption is total. In the final scene, unaware that his daughter has become a heroin addict, he delivers another speech indicating his complete acceptance of their dishonesty: 'We've had our share of troubles and we've seen them off. And together, I can promise you this, we will continue to see them off – whoever they are and wherever they come from.'[50]

Any resemblance Jack may by this point bear to a mafia godfather is intentional, for the methods by which he might 'see off' any future troubles are bound to be underhand. His story serves only to emphasise the futility of idealism in a world ruled by commerce. In fact, this is not just a play about the assimilation of an honest man into an evil world; given its historical context, it's hard not to read it also as an attack on Mrs Thatcher's ambition to make businessmen of us all. If this is the least reserved, and most sardonic, of Ayckbourn's 1980s tragedies, that's largely because of its equation of business with crime and corruption.

The Revengers' Comedies (1989) is less bleak. Like Guy in *A Chorus of Disapproval*, their protagonist, Henry Bell, works for a multinational; or, as he tells Karen, a young lady also trying to commit suicide on Albert Bridge:

HENRY: Multi. Multi. Multi.
KAREN: Polluting the rivers, poisoning the atmosphere and secretly funding right-wing revolutionaries.
HENRY: Those are the chaps.
KAREN: Why did they fire you?

HENRY: Oh. All the jargon. Redefining the job profile. Rationalizing the department. Restructuring the management team. Which essentially meant either get promoted or – get out. And, innocent that I was, so certain that I'd been doing a good job, I sat there fully expecting to be promoted.[51]

The corrupt political environment which these characters inhabit is instantly recognisable as that of the late 1980s – even the Iran-Contra scandal gets a mention. As usual, Ayckbourn uses it as the backdrop for a discussion of ethics on a more immediate, individual level. In fact, the relation of worldly matters – particularly business – to personal morality is a central theme of the play. Henry's innocent belief that he will get on merely by working well is starkly opposed to the essential inhumanity of organisational politics – a feature thinly disguised by the jargon used to justify his redundancy.

Like so many of Ayckbourn's protagonists during the 1980s, Henry is an innocent in a corrupt world. Only belatedly does he realise that success is granted to those who break the rules: 'You've also got to be working the system. Chatting up the right people. Buying the drinks that matter. Arranging the cosy little dinner with the boss's P.A. Taking the right lift at the right moment with the right people. Going down – hallo, Mr Pride, sir – fancy bumping into you, remember me? Losing the right game of squash. Missing the right putt. Winning the right rubber. Licking the right shoes. Sending the right Christmas cards. Driving the right car. Choosing the right suit. Wearing the right bloody underwear. Screwing the right secretary'.[52] The losers in the society Henry inhabits are those for whom love is more than a means of self-advancement. All human activity, from the most banal to the most personal, has been debased to the level of a game in which worldly success is all. It is the same ethos as that postulated by Jerome in *Henceforward . . .*, where love is merely a piece of software, to be retrieved (or deleted) at will.

It was Howard Brenton who noted that 'There is an infinite variety of ways of making theatre, but only one theme which, inevitably, Aeschylus was onto – it's simply "how can we live justly?"'[53] What makes *The Revengers' Comedies* comparatively optimistic is that it attempts to respond to precisely that question. In the wake of a series of dramatic works in which love is disempowered, mocked and rejected, *The Revengers' Comedies* attempts to revalue it, to redefine it in the face of the spiritual desolation that epitomised the 1980s. Henry and Karen are thus allowed remission from a watery grave so that they can attempt to find a way of life that transcends the degraded morays of Thatcherite Britain, and that reasserts some concept of humane conduct. Karen is the first to provide an answer:

KAREN: Revenge, HenryBell, revenge.
HENRY: Revenge?
KAREN: (*Excitedly*) That's why we're being kept alive, HenryBell, you and I. Why we weren't allowed to die. We're unquiet spirits, if you like, with unfinished business. The wrongs that have been done to us have got to be put right. We're never going to rest, either of us, until we've done that.[54]

Karen assumes that she and Henry are doomed; they are 'being kept alive', 'unquiet spirits' who will die after they've revenged each others' wrongs. Her proposal is flawed by its acceptance of the values that have destroyed their will to live in the first place – and it comes as no surprise that, by the end of the play, she has found no reason to delay her suicide any longer. The revenge motif is borrowed from Patricia Highsmith's *Strangers on a Train*, and Karen shares with Bruno, the effete, well-to-do bachelor of Highsmith's novel, a deranged psychology. But Ayckbourn incorporates these features into a serious debate of his own.

Karen cold-bloodedly leads several executives in Henry's multinational to either collapse or kill themselves in order to fulfil what she regards herself as her side of a bargain. She becomes upset when Henry fails to fulfil his by falling in love with, rather than murdering, her neighbour and sexual rival, Imogen Staxton-Billing:

KAREN: That is entirely contrary to what we agreed. I'm afraid you're not able to do that, HenryBell, that is breaking the rules. I'm sorry, I can't allow you to break the rules. Out. Fault. Out.
HENRY: Karen, I'm not talking about rules. I'm talking about real life – this is real life -
KAREN: (*Blazing*) And I'm talking about rules which are a bloody sight more important –
HENRY: Karen, Karen. This is reality. Real, do you understand? It is not a game. Life is not a game, Karen.

KAREN: (*Quietly*) Who told you that?
HENRY: It happens to be the case. There's a much bigger board,
         for one thing. People keep stealing your counters and
         changing the rules. Life's a lot more complicated and a
         good deal harder to play. Take it from me.[55]

Only by his acceptance that life is essentially anarchic, innately
resistant to laws, has Henry reconciled himself to injustice. His
earlier innocence gave rise to a rulebound philosophy whereby he
believed that hard work would necessarily lead to promotion.
Karen, on the other hand, will never outgrow her need for a world
governed by invisible structures. The damned of Ayckbourn's
world are imprisoned by abstraction: Susan in *Woman in Mind*,
Jerome in *Henceforward* . . . and Karen in *The Revengers' Comedies*.
All are confined by abstract ideas that lead, ultimately, to their
undoing.

Inappropriate though it may seem to intellectualise about an
essentially anti-intellectual posture, this feature of Ayckbourn's
work has vital implications for an understanding of his work. Of the
dramatists discussed here, he is, surprisingly, the only one whose
response to Thatcherism might be described as genuinely post-
romantic. Rousseau provided Wordsworth and Coleridge with their
rallying-cry when he wrote: 'Man was born free, and he is
everywhere in chains.'[56] He assumes that, though naturally well-
intentioned, our moral nature is thwarted by the routine injustices of
the world. On that foundation a grand edifice of political thought
has been constructed to help retrieve our supposed birthright of
benevolence and virtue.

Recognising that it was vain to long for an ethical golden age that
never existed, Ayckbourn stumbled on an insight well-suited to the
turbulent change of the late 1980s. He saw that the chains that
destroy our liberty are neither forged by bad governments, nor may
they be shaken off: *they are what we are*. Despite the wishes of latter-
day romantics, Mrs Thatcher was one of the most popular political
leaders in British history – why? Partly because she legitimised what
was already there. In *The Revengers' Comedies*, Karen's failure to see
beyond the rules that govern her life leaves her, at the end of the
play, with no option but to commit suicide. Throughout his work,
Ayckbourn compels us to confront a nature that has always been
fallen, as seen in the canonisation of Vic Parks; Guy's betrayal of
Dafydd; Susan's repudiation of her loving husband; Jerome's

abandonment of his wife and child; and Jack McCracken's capitulation to the criminality of his business associates.

On the other hand, Henry is redeemed through his relationship with Imogen. The outside world is lawless, but he knows that love carries its own obligations, and is strong enough to fulfil them – as when he tells Imogen about the revenge pact, even though it might imperil their relationship. Henry's moral courage enables *The Revengers' Comedies* to reclaim some of the hope relinquished in earlier works. We can be true, we can recover our lost innocence, we can indulge our romantic aspirations, providing that we do not deceive ourselves into thinking that such aspirations are governed by absolutes.

All of which had little bearing on the box-office failure of Ayckbourn's London production of *The Revengers' Comedies*. One of the penalties of being regarded (however unfairly) as a comic playwright is that audiences are reluctant to apply themselves to your work in quite the same manner that they might that of other writers – for instance, by attending the theatre on two consecutive nights, as was necessary for those who wished to see both parts of the play.

If *Time of My Life* (1992), Ayckbourn's most recent success in the West End, is one of his darkest works, it consolidates the practicality so typical of his vision. Its most obvious precursor is Priestley's *An Inspector Calls* (1946), with which it shares a basic conceit: that the apparent warmth and generosity of a well-to-do family is stripped away to expose their true inhumanity and selfishness. Like Priestley, Ayckbourn sets his play in the provinces, and takes as its focus a celebration, in this case, the birthday of Laura Stratton. Around this one evening he reveals the past and future by a clever use of flashbacks and flash-forwards. Laura's husband, Gerry, is a wealthy local businessman, who has taken the family out to a restaurant for her party. As they begin their meal he makes a short speech:

> in life, you get moments – just occasionally which you can positively identify as being among the happy moments. They come up occasionally, even take you by surprise, and sometimes you're so busy worrying about tomorrow or thinking about yesterday that you tend to miss out on them altogether. I'd like to hope tonight might be one such moment. And if it is – let's not miss out on this one, alright? All that really means is, enjoy yourselves.[57]

Gerry's 'happy moment' may stop short of the transcendental longing behind Wordsworth's spots of time – the emotional experience that, for the poet of *The Prelude*, possessed a 'fructifying' virtue for the human spirit – but it does establish a romantic impulse even among the practicalities of life. A builder's merchant by trade, Gerry invites us, in simple, down-to-earth language, to step outside worldly cares and surrender ourselves to the moment. This is the philosophy that informs Ayckbourn's work. If Paradise exists, it is to be found on earth, in our dealings with those closest to us, rather than in art or abstraction. Unfortunately, Gerry is to be deprived even of this.

The play's structure is circular, so that his speech, which takes place at the beginning of the dinner-party, is actually performed at the end of the play, by which time it has been thoroughly undermined. To believe that his family could be capable of happiness, Gerry must be either self-deceiving, or morally blind, or both. We have seen how Glyn and Adam, his sons, have been psychologically crippled by their overbearing mother, who detests one and adores the other. We have seen how she destroys Adam's attempts to establish relationships with women, and how her hatred has made Glyn weak and feckless. Glyn's wife Stephanie describes her, correctly, as 'a selfish, self-centred, destructive old woman'.[58]

Most disturbingly of all, we have seen Laura admit to Gerry an infidelity with his brother, David – a revelation that upsets him deeply:

LAURA: Oh, don't be so melodramatic.
GERRY: I've reason to be, haven't I? I discover, after thiry-two years, my whole marriage is based on a lie. I've been betrayed by my wife – with my own brother . . . My whole personal life been made a mockery . . .
LAURA: (*Impatiently*) Oh, for God's sake. Fifteen minutes. That's all it was. In 1974. A month before he died, poor bugger. From the little pleasure we had from it, it probably helped him on his way.
GERRY: God, you're a cold woman sometimes, aren't you?
LAURA: It's the truth. Come on, don't be so stupid. It was nothing.
GERRY: Then why bother telling me if it was nothing?
LAURA: I don't know. I thought it might amuse you.[59]

In his personal life Gerry is a moral absolutist, so dependent on the rules that establish the outward respectability of his married life that he is unable to cope when they break down; Othello is destabilised in a similar way. At an opposite extreme, Laura takes a hard-boiled, materialistic view of her fling, unmoved either by its proximity to David's death, or by her husband's distress. To her, it really 'was nothing'. Why bother telling him? Her malign glee confirms that it is an act of hatred. Not that she is totally without justification; Gerry has already admitted that he used to hit her.[60] But Ayckbourn characterises him less by violence than by the ideals that govern his family life.

For Gerry, the real cause for celebration that evening is the reconcilation of Glyn and his wife Stephanie. After an affair with another woman, Glyn has returned to his family; while in the Gents, Gerry makes him promise not to leave them again, and is sufficiently self-deceiving to believe that this will be enough to make his son change his ways. The same quality enables Glyn to kid himself that he has not broken his promise even after leaving Stephanie a second time: 'I mean I know I haven't been actually living with you, but I haven't walked out on you, have I? Not technically. I've still been looking after you. From a distance. If you appreciate the distinction.'[61] Glyn's inability to confront the truth is inherited from his father. Gerry convinces himself that Laura 'wanted grandchildren more than she wanted children',[62] even though he is aware of her hatred for Glyn and his son.[63]

Unsurprisingly, Glyn is the only member of the family with whom Gerry's pre-prandial speech registered; he recalls it, years later, just after Stephanie asks him for a divorce:

> well, the point is – I doubt if any of us knew it at the time – it was something Dad said, actually – that was probably one of the best, the happiest moments of our lives. Only the trouble with those sorts of moments is that you seldom ever realize what they are – until they've gone. Do you see? I mean very rarely do you find yourself saying to yourself, I am happy *now*. Sometimes you say, I was happy *then*. Or sometimes even, I will be happy *when* . . . But rarely do you get to realize it *now*. If you know what I mean.[64]

His memory has worked a subtle alteration on his father's speech, so that he believes that Gerry identified that evening as one of the happiest of their lives. In fact, Gerry said, 'I'd like to hope tonight

might be one such moment.' As the audience realises, Laura's birthday party was full of strains and anxieties that culminated with tragedy. But Glyn has idealised his father's remarks, so that they refer not so much to pleasure as to regret – specifically, that arising from his abandonment of his family. What his memory of Gerry's speech reveals is that he is too self-deceiving to know what happiness is. 'Who the hell ever knows when they're happy?' he asks, 'I don't know.'[65]

The biggest casualty of Gerry's deluded nature is himself. Told to calm down for fear of giving himself a heart attack after Laura discloses her infidelity, he retorts that 'I won't be the one who drops dead. Have no fear about that. Whoever he is, he'll be the one that drops dead because I'll murder the bastard. I'll kill him and I'll thrash the living daylights out of you.'[66] That the culprit, his brother David, is already dead, only compounds his suffering. His anger is true to the psychology of jealousy, and to literary representations of it. Like Othello, Gerry depends on the security of his personal life in a world shaken by uncertainty. (Incidentally, the play's setting – that of Britain in the early 1990s – is particularly useful for Ayckbourn's purposes. Thanks to the recession, Gerry's company, one of the largest and most successful in the region, is on the verge of financial ruin, kept afloat only by Gerry's crooked dealings. As Glyn remarks after his death, 'God knows what the old boy was playing at. Money missing from here. Money deposited there with no record at all of how it got there. Where it came from. I don't know how he got away with it.'[67]) The sudden loss of emotional security proves too much, and the ultimate irony of Gerry's threat to murder his wife's lover is that he deliberately crashes their car into a tree on the way home from dinner, killing himself and injuring her. The self-deceived of Ayckbourn's dramas are always self-destructive.

Few dramatists could handle a plot like this without slipping into melodrama; Ayckbourn pulls it off partly by his convincing treatment of Laura's malignity. If Gerry resembles Othello, she makes a good Iago, taunting him with details of her affair, forcing him to guess her lover's identity. After which she tells him that she thought it would amuse him: 'Well, it was long enough ago. (*Laughing*) It was very funny, actually . . .'[68] Laura has no conscience, and owes her survival to a dedicated materialism. She is also violent. At one point she tells Gerry that she was attracted to him when they first met by the fact that she thought 'You were – dangerous. So dangerous.'[69] She saw off her rivals with a 'quick word in the toilet and a bottle of nail polish remover',[70] and uses similar tactics in dealing with Adam's new girlfriend, Maureen.

Laura sees Maureen as a rival for her son's affections, and on the evening of the dinner, at their first encounter, wastes no time in dissuading him from seeing her:

LAURA: Maureen's a young woman with a serious personal
        problem and a shrewd eye for the main chance . . .
ADAM: I'm not listening to this –
LAURA: Adam . . .
ADAM: I'm not. I'm sorry.
LAURA: Adam, do you want to break your father's heart?
        Because that's what you're going to end up doing . . .
ADAM: Oh, bollocks . . .
LAURA: You want to kill your own father, go ahead . . .
ADAM: Oh, bugger off![71]

Aware of Adam's desperate need for his father's approval, Laura blackmails him with the threat of permanently displeasing Gerry, even to the point of destroying his will to live. It is a calculated act of manipulation, all the more shocking for the fact that it is Laura who turns out to be the cause of Gerry's death. Even so, she uses it to pressurise Adam even further; Stephanie tells to Glyn that 'Apparently your mother told him that Maureen's behaviour on her birthday evening upset his father so deeply, that was the reason he got drunk and drove off the road.'[72] This is one of the most sinister disclosures in the play. Like Iago, Laura is a hardened opportunist, ruthless in her exploitation of others' weaknesses. Knowing who was really responsible, she blamed Gerry's death on an innocent party as a means of keeping her son to herself. In *An Inspector Calls*, Priestley allows his characters to prevent Eva Smith's suicide, for which they might have been jointly responsible; Ayckbourn is less merciful. In his world angels do not masquerade as policemen, intervening in human affairs so as to avert disaster. *Time of My Life* is an accomplished tragedy not just because Laura effectively kills her husband and gets away with it, but because she succeeds in using it as a means of possessing her son for ever. By the end, Adam is living at home, without either a girlfriend or a steady job, reduced to looking after his mother's dogs.

But he is also culpable for failing to resist her. He knows better than to believe that Maureen is interested only in the Stratton fortune. Ayckbourn reveals how she met Adam by accident, and grew attached to him before she learned that he belonged to a wealthy family. When Adam tells her, she responds with characteristic honesty: 'I didn't come out because you were rich . . . because I didn't know who you were when I said yes and it wouldn't have made any difference even if I had done'.[73] One of the waiters in the restaurant calls Maureen, 'Deveena Madametta'[74] – a judgement which turns out to be correct. She is the most virtuous character in the play, and is undeceived about others' motives. Early in her relationship with Adam she realises that he is ashamed of her:

MAUREEN: It's all become so – important, hasn't it?

ADAM: How do you mean? You mean to you? Important to you?

MAUREEN: No. To you.

ADAM: Me? I don't care. I don't give a stuff.

MAUREEN: You do give a stuff, that's the point. You give a huge stuff. I wish you didn't.

ADAM: I don't. I do what I like. I always have done. I don't take any notice of them. I don't care what they think.

MAUREEN: But you want them to like me, don't you?

ADAM: I don't mind either way . . .

MAUREEN: You need them to approve –

ADAM: I really don't –

MAUREEN: You do, Adam. You do, you know.

ADAM: I don't know why you should think that.

MAUREEN: Because you keep going on about it. 'Maureen, when you meet them, don't say this, will you? Don't say that.'

ADAM: When did I – ?

MAUREEN: 'Don't wear that, will you, they won't approve of that. Be careful not to swear, will you? Don't say condoms, pessaries and penis in front of my mother, will you?'[75]

Maureen sees through Adam's self-deception, and is strong enough to confront him with it. But he refuses to admit that he is dependent on his mother's approval for everything, and eventually she capitulates to his anxieties. In the weeks preceding the dinner, he tones down her 'full exotic self'[76] and forces her to adopt the manner of a different person. It is an impossible task, for no woman could be acceptable to Laura.

The opening scene is set at the end of the meal, by which time Maureen is, uncharacteristically, drunk. Not until the end of the play, which is set at the beginning of the evening, do we see why. Moments after their introduction, Maureen reveals that she lives in Harwick Road:

ADAM: Maureen lives the other end. By the canal.
LAURA: Oh, in one of those lovely little cottages?
MAUREEN: Yes.
LAURA: By the canal?
MAUREEN: Yes.
LAURA: Lovely old places. Aren't they damp, at all?
MAUREEN: No, not really, no.
LAURA: Amazing. I'd have thought being that near water. (*To* STEPHANIE) I don't think I could live near canals. I'd be frightened of rats and things, wouldn't you?
STEPHANIE: Well . . .
MAUREEN: We don't have rats . . .
ADAM: They don't have rats, Mother . . .
LAURA: Oh really. I thought that's where rats lived. Near canals . . .
ADAM: Mother . . .
MAUREEN: They can live anywhere. Can rats.
LAURA: Really?
MAUREEN: Wherever there's dirt. Or filth. Or any sort of shit for that matter.[77]

This important exchange reveals that Maureen is rejected because she is the only character strong enough to stand up to Laura. Her reference to 'any sort of shit' is not just a rebuttal of the jibe about rats, but indicates her instinctive opinion of Laura herself – a point that takes us to the thematic heart of the play. The ability to separate good from evil is vital to our survival; Maureen possesses it and is brave enough to act upon it. By contrast, the men of the Stratton family are flawed by a fundamental moral blindness, such that they are unable to recognise Laura for what she is. In different ways, she has managed to cripple each of them, either psychologically or emotionally or both.

Moral confusion is a feature of Shakespearean tragedy; *Othello* is unable to tell right from wrong as he smothers Desdemona. However, it is the truth that compels Gerry to drive his car off the road. For the first time, he has understood the extent of his wife's evil, and realises that he must kill her even if it means killing himself. Shakespeare brings matters to a satisfying climax at which, providing we remain sympathetic to Othello's claims that he is behaving justly as he kills Desdemona, we may experience a tragic precipitation of emotion. Such neat resolutions, as Ayckbourn knows, are the stuff of fiction. Gerry's death is given only the most casual mention – neither of his sons, significantly, expresses any grief; while Laura, the villain of the piece, is allowed to survive beyond the end of the play so that she can wreck the life of her youngest son.

While it would be an error to overlook the humour in this play, *Time of My Life* is finally very bleak indeed. In *An Inspector Calls*, Priestley gives the selfish, destructive Birlings a second chance, the implication being that it is possible to learn from one's mistakes. Our moral blindness, he believed, can be overcome, and people can learn to behave decently to one another. Ayckbourn is a realist, not disposed, as at the end of *A Chorus of Disapproval*, to pander to our wishes. There is no reprieve for his characters; as in life, they have only one chance.

The play's bleakness is qualified only by the benevolent hope, expressed by Gerry, for those moments 'which you can positively identify as being among the happy moments'. It may not sound like much, but its virtue lies in its pragmatism and its belief in small, everyday pleasures. But Gerry is unredeemed by this conviction – in fact, as I have suggested, it rebounds ironically in view of what happens later. It is, however, the most Ayckbourn is willing to concede, and is typical of the reserved, conditional stance of the plays of the 1980s and early 1990s.

Its practicality also underlies his recent comment on *A Small Family Business*: 'What the play's really about is the virtual non-existence of set moral codes any more, and the fallacy of trying to live by one. I think the only thing we can do – and in a way cannot help doing – is to make up our own moral codes as we go along.'[78] There are bad ways and good ways of doing this: Jack's submission to his family's shady business ethics in *A Small Family Business* stands at one extreme; at the other, Henry in *The Revengers' Comedies* finds a secure moral locus through his love for Imogen Staxton-Billing. True love is the best way of all – and it is the one thing denied to the men of the Stratton family. That is what makes *Time of My Life* tragic and *The Revengers' Comedies* comic.

Ayckbourn's position is not so different from the tight-lipped imperative behind Larkin's *The Mower*, also framed by intimations of mortality. Both writers acknowledge the attractions of romanticism, but neither can stomach the self-deception which it entails. Both stake out a fallback position justified by its eminent practicality. Nuances of romanticism may persist, but survive only in the most localised of contexts, that of the individual's conduct towards those around him. Larkin places particular emphasis on 'kind', drawing not only on its meaning of 'benevolent, generous, affectionate', but on its Old English root, *gecynde*, 'natural, native':[79]

> The mower stalled, twice; kneeling, I found
> A hedgehog jammed up against the blades,
> Killed. It had been in the long grass.
>
> I had seen it before, and even fed it, once.
> Now I had mauled its unobtrusive world
> Unmendably. Burial was no help:
>
> Next morning I got up and it did not.
> The first day after a death, the new absence
> Is always the same; we should be careful
>
> Of each other, we should be kind
> While there is still time.[80]

8

Epilogue

In *The Second Wave* (1971), John Russell Taylor concluded that there was 'a certain consistency' in recent drama:

> an anarchic spirit seems to be abroad. Sometimes, though not always, it is an anarchism born of despair – despair at the decay of forms, the inescapable disharmony between man and his environment, the tragic inability of man to come to terms directly with society as it now is, with scientific development, with the uncontrollable forces within his own nature; man's inability to live happily either in chains or free, either with religion or without it.[1]

The diversity of subjects and writers in Taylor's volume pays tribute to a healthily productive theatre world, one in which there was a great deal more going on than there is now. The chief reason for today's comparative dearth of talent is the recent political changes described in the Introduction. Independent theatre companies are finding it increasingly difficult to survive, and there is far less drama produced cheaply for television today than in 1971; the 30 or 45 minute television play is all but extinct. 'If I started now', Potter has commented, 'where would I get the chance? Where today is the single play? It is formula-ridden TV. The pressure now is to maximise the audience.'[2] As a result, there are fewer outlets for the work either of new writers, or of established ones.

That contraction augurs badly for the next 20 years; where will the writers of the next century come from? In 1971 Taylor found consolation in the observation that written drama 'throws up enough new excitements, enough worthwhile new talents, to justify its continued survival and to perpetuate itself.'[3] I doubt whether it will continue to do so for much longer; the day will come when the talents nurtured by the appetite for theatrical experiment during the 1960s and 1970s will have run their course, and at that point live theatre will come to depend even more than it does at present on revivals and rehashed versions of the classics.[4] There will be fewer

141

writers, and those that emerge will concentrate on television and
film, media that will consolidate their hold on the market.

The anarchy of subject-matter noted by Taylor was the result
partly of the intellectual exuberance of the 1960s – a decade of
dissent which threw up many issues and causes that worked their
way into literary works of the time. That energy has long since
waned, and fringe theatre is no longer an arena for debate. This may
help to explain why the anxieties that Taylor detected in 1971 have
become dominant. Writers that survived that period, such as those
profiled in this book, have sought to accommodate a greater realism
in their work, a realism informed by an essentially tragic sense. Thus
recent political developments at home and abroad give added
weight to the darker side of Brenton's *Berlin Bertie* and Hare's *The
Absence of War*. All the same, current affairs cannot account fully for
that intensified sense of reality.

'In a world of dishonest people, could we recognize an honest
man?' This theme has always interested Ayckbourn – and, as
Brenton notes, it is the basic concern of all dramatic writers – but it
has become more pressing in the last two decades. One of the buried
themes of this volume is self-destructiveness. Irene in *A Lady of
Letters*, Jessica in *Blackeyes*, Harry in *Hidden Laughter*, Nicole and
Raymond in *Hess is Dead*, Janetta in *Heading Home* and Gerry in *Time
of My Life* – all suffer from a moral blindness that is self-destructive
in its effects. Janetta is fortunate merely in ending up with feelings
of regret; Irene goes to jail; Harry loses his family; and Nicole,
Raymond and Gerry lose their lives. They epitomise a tendency
deeply embedded within the human psyche, one which is
inextricably connected to our moral vision. In their different ways,
these writers warn against the deceptiveness or indifference that
may seal our fate. Auden cancelled one of his poems, 'September 1,
1939', from his published works, as it contained a line which he felt
in retrospect to be untrue: 'We must love one another or die'. At
moments of crisis, however, such sentiments often seem to possess
an urgency lacking in more realistic assessments of the world. There
is a sense, in the work of the writers examined here, that we are
living through troubled times, and that such aspirations as these
answer a vital need, even if they are false. This has produced a
tension that David Hare noted in his own work as long ago as 1977:

I believe in what used to be called socialist realism, that you
should try to show how things are and how things could be. Plays

have tension if you do both; if you only show how things are it's boring and if you only show how they could be, it's strident and hollow.[5]

The balance between wish-fulfilment and realism is never constant, and in recent years things as they are have impinged on each writer's vision. It has led to a sense of closure, as the playwrights discussed here have slowed their pace of work during the 1990s. Brenton, Bennett and Gray have produced nothing for the stage for at least two years at the time of writing; Potter is shortly to die. Hare is probably the most hopeful, but a sense of loss, even to the point of grief, pervades even his work, as in *The Secret Rapture* or *The Absence of War*.

It is no accident that this change of mood has coincided with a crisis in arts funding, and especially that of the theatre. The resultant changes have prompted established writers to become more insistent in defining their role and the part theatre can play in the world. If the ferment of activity in written drama during the 1960s and early 1970s is not to be seen again, some consolation may be drawn from the renewed emphasis placed by dramatists on morality – a subject that takes us, not just to the roots of the art, but to the question of our survival. 'If we do not live in such a way that the free self-realization of each is achieved in and through the free self-realization of all', Terry Eagleton has suggested, 'then we are very likely to destroy ourselves as a species'.[6] Grounds for hope may be found in the joint conviction that ethics are the true subject of drama (whether live, filmed or televised) and that playwrights still have much to say about what constitutes just behaviour. Whether, in coming years, they will be able to resist the despair detected by John Russell Taylor is another matter.

Appendix:
An Interview with
Alan Ayckbourn

Given Ayckbourn's numerous published utterances – most notably in Ian Watson's *Conversations with Ayckbourn* (2nd edn, 1988), and to a lesser extent in Malcolm Page's *File on Ayckbourn* (1989) – the reader might well ask, why another interview? Despite the excellence of both Watson and Page, neither of them pursues the issue of Ayckbourn as a moral writer – one central to an understanding of his work.[1]

At the end of his year-long tenure of the Cameron Mackintosh Chair of Contemporary Drama at St Catherine's College, Oxford, 1991–2, Ayckbourn agreed to clarify for me, in conversation, his preoccupations as a moral writer. We met at the Old Parsonage Hotel, Oxford, on 5 December 1992, where the following discussion was recorded. Since I have drawn several times on this transcript in the course of my chapter on Ayckbourn, it seemed appropriate to present it here.

Duncan Wu: What ought we to make of the last scene of *A Chorus of Disapproval*, in which Guy is hugged by the rest of the cast and everyone makes up?[2] Is it a sign of hope?

Alan Ayckbourn: Well, the play runs parallel to *The Beggar's Opera*, and there's a wonderful moment in *The Beggar's Opera* where they say 'If you want a happy ending, you can have it'. And I wanted the same with *Chorus*. So that's what happens at the point where the play would normally come round to the end of the flashback: I change course, and say, 'If you want a happy ending, here it is.'

But what I liked is the slightly cynical way in which Gay uses the device – if the town wants a happy ending, we'll tag one on. It's from years of hearing the public (not so much the critics) saying to me, 'I think you could have made it a bit happier at the end'. I thought, 'I know exactly how Gay feels'. Okay, snip! The man turns round and he's terribly nice.

DW: He's been behaving like a total bastard throughout, though.

AA: I don't think so. He's an innocent.

DW: Really innocent?

AA: Well, he's not by any means beyond criticism, because you might argue, from the way he gets involved with two or three women, that he's quite happy to sit back and let events flow in his favour.

It's my theory that if a man the stature of Jesus Christ came back now, we'd all be trying to figure his angle. We'd all be saying, 'He must be up to something.' This is true even in a town like Scarborough. I think people now know what I'm doing there. But a lot of the sharper members of the community – the amusement arcade boys, for instance – they never knew what I was doing there. The papers said, 'Here's a guy who's very successful', and yet I was there running a very small theatre, and they couldn't figure my angle. In the end they figured me for Mr Big, that I obviously had some operation going that was of such scale – a major importation from Columbia Pictures, or something – that it was unfigurable.

Similarly, in *Chorus*, the characters tend to see themselves mirrored in Guy. The fact that he demurs or doesn't react in the way they expect – far from making them think he's an idiot – leads them to think that he's deeper than they thought. In a world of dishonest people, could we recognise an honest man? (Hopefully, that's actually a rather jaded view.)

DW: Which leads me to ask whether we should read the play as a critique of Thatcherism.

AA: Well, it's a critique of a society that's Mammon-based, I suppose. And it certainly applied to the Thatcher era, as did *A Small Family Business*. But I was writing about the subject long before Mrs Thatcher, and it's aimed at more than just her. *Absurd Person Singular* is also about avarice and greed – a lot of my plays are about the seven deadly sins!

It's my theory that you can become amazingly rich if you have a modicum of intelligence, an incredible obsession and determination, can dispense with a few niceties like other people's feelings, and have a certain ruthlessness. The nice people, the gentle people, the people I like, are the ones that – well, I wouldn't say they give it all to Oxfam, but they don't go through with it for various reasons.

DW: People like Dafydd, I guess.

AA: Yes. Who I love very much. He's a terrible man in some ways. He resembles many of the people I knew when I was young, a type you don't often meet professionally. They're characterised by an obsessive commitment, a desperate love for the theatre.

When Michael Gambon was doing *A Chorus*, and I was directing him at the National Theatre, we gave Dafydd this tiny house in which he lived, with little rooms, much too small for him. He's only ever fully alive when he's in that big auditorium. He's pacing around and this is his land, his realm. There he's master of his own domain. But at home he's like this big animal that's been shut in a very small crate, bashing his head against the walls. I always told Gambon to pace around inside the house, constantly meeting walls, never quite sure of the architecture of his house. He's always doing very big, passionate gestures in much too small a space.

DW: You mention the seven deadly sins, and you are a very moral writer. But *A Small Family Business* seems to suggest that there are no moral absolutes. How do we know right from wrong in your work?

AA: In *A Small Family Business* the absolutes are felt to be impossible to achieve. I mean, who hasn't done something in their lives that makes them blush – lifted a book out of Smith's, done something in some drunken spree (or even sober)? The point I was trying to make is that although we're all prone to this, there's a direct link between a tiny crime and a big crime. It is a dangerous slope that you step on if you condone one crime – one racial incident, one anything. Again, at the centre of the play is this totally honest man, a rather belligerent man, Jack, who's almost impossible to live with. He's a cross between Don Quixote and St George, always going off looking for dragons.

The mark in that play is his first speech to his family, which is awkward.[3] He talks rather self-consciously about moral values in a very clumsy way, and he phrases it wrongly – and I deliberately wrote it with hesitations and repetitions. He talks about things that in decent society aren't talked about, like having principles. Everyone nods and looks a bit embarrassed and wishes he'd shut up, because they'd rather get on with the party – and also it's painfully close to the bone because everyone in the room is a crook! But by the end of the play he's mastered the speak, and he's giving the smooth politician/mafioso speech about family and ties; it's all very smooth and honed, says almost the same things as before, only much more briefly, swiftly, and shallowly.[4] The movement has been very small in real terms. He's shifted from being a totally honest man to being a corrupt man. But without being aware that it's happened to him. The moral of that play is that we can change without realising it, if we compromise on what we believe in. And we are a nation of compromisers. It's that combined with our apathy that has saved us from doing the unspeakable. I wouldn't put it down to moral fibre so much as a reluctance to leave the pub. I can't imagine, for instance, our farmers ever behaving like the French farmers. And hopefully our politics aren't quite at the stage that German politics have reached. But it's dangerous to assume that they won't. We're not immune. We might suddenly find ourselves there, simply by taking no action.

DW: Should I be looking for a consistent moral core to your plays, or is that the wrong way of thinking about them?

AA: You only find out about your work from what people say. All I do is write it. But Peter Hall once said to me that he thought I was a modern Ben Jonson, that I write morality plays – I mean plays about good and evil. I don't consciously set out to do it, but I suppose there is an inevitable sense of justice in my work: as ye sow so shall ye reap. That sort of thing is quite often in my work. That is a recurring theme.

DW: I notice that in your work there's often a good way of living and a bad way of living. In *Henceforward . . .* we know that the good way of living is for the man to go back to his wife and child, but he narrowly misses that and goes back to the bad way of living. I don't want to schematise it, but you frequently present your protagonists with moral choices. In *A Small Family Business* Jack knows what the right way to live is, but he gets sucked into the wrong way.

AA: It's not easy is what I'm saying. At every stage I wanted Jack to be presented with tough choices. In the first case it's either take the guy's offer or have your daughter prosecuted and possibly appear in a juvenile court. Of course he wants to protect the kid, even though he's almost strong enough to say 'No, she must be punished.' But then his whole family come back and say, 'Can't have that.' Once he's capitulated to that then every corrupt decision is justified.

Henceforward . . . is slightly different. It's not exactly autobiographical but it is the closest I've come to writing about the so-called creative artist, and feelings about using your life, recycling in dramatic form experiences you may have shared with other people. It's a difficult thing to discuss if you're writing about a writer because they just sit and write. There's nothing to look at really, except a man with a pen or a word-processor. And even watching composers compose isn't much fun. (I know that Hollywood have tried raindrops falling on Beethoven's music and so on.) But I thought it was more interesting once you'd got sampled sound, making it possible to see the act of creation. One didn't need to be convinced that it was brilliant; all one wanted to know was that the composer was obsessed with his work.

The irony of the play is that he's obsessed with the very thing he's destroying in his own life. He wants to produce a piece of music that will zock people into loving each other – pure subliminal advertising for the good life. Then there's the meeting at the end where old ironsides – his wife, Corinna, who, out of defence I think, is as tough as old bricks – cracks in half and shows all to him. I said to the actress playing her, 'Never should a woman have said "I love you" with more conviction than this woman does; never has a man been quite so loved with no holds barred; and never has he turned away a bigger bunch of flowers.' Because instead of accepting it he recognises it as the very sound he wanted for his piece.[5]

DW: That's very painful. Is it tragedy?

AA: It is, it is. His family almost certainly dies as a result, and he's left with a piece of useless junk, really. I think what the play says is that drama, or any art, can't exist outside society.

We live in a society that puts art outside. It's a sort of twin culture. You've got so-called art that everybody can understand, like *EastEnders* – things that are popular. And then you've got after ten o'clock art, which is often theatre. In Scarborough the other day someone said to me, 'I never knew that theatre was like this, I thought everyone would be in evening dress.' Well, outside Covent Garden, when was the last time I saw an audience in evening dress? And that's what *Henceforward* . . .'s about: the danger of putting art away from people. I always say to anyone who writes for our theatre in Scarborough: 'It's got to be relevant. I don't care what you want to say but it's got to relate to these people.' And the bigger the subject, the more personally involved you've got to get them. Because most people in this country can wriggle free from most hooks; if it's happening further than 20 yards away, forget it. Although it's true that I write about individuals rather than issues, you could say, for 'a small family business' read 'a whole nation state'. It isn't that it's just a family, it goes further and wider than that. In dealing with a family, I try to indicate that it happens at 44 Hollyhock Street; it's not something cooked up by Mrs Thatcher and a whole load of people who I don't know anything about.

When Mrs T. was around, and people were complaining about her, I always said that she embodies what the majority of this country believe, and aim for, and strive for. She's there because they put her there, or somebody put her there. I never met anyone who voted for her, and yet a lot of people did, and a lot of people made a lot of money out of it. You get what you deserve. She was our representative on earth, really – what we all jointly created.

DW: Do you feel that the ethics of the Thatcherite society had any effect on your work?

AA: You can't reduce everything in the end to a profit sheet. And that's the legacy we've got in the arts. But not just in the arts.

One is aware of a tremendous levelling. Take a small town like Scarborough. We're looking for money at the theatre, just to survive. We've been told, 'Go out into the market-place; no more direct handouts from the government' (although they will continue, but for how long one doesn't really know). 'Be prepared to generate your own income, and hassle local businesses', and so on. But you find yourself standing in the queue with the local hospice, with schools, with sick children, with all sorts of huge emotive causes – the dying, the young and the old and the homeless. You've all got the same tin. And in a sense it puts things that the British are naturally suspicious about – art, culture – in a very vulnerable position. It's just unfair to expect us to compete with a hospice. I mean, people are going to go where their hearts are hit, and a production of *Hamlet* next month is neither here nor there. But it is here or there because I really do believe that, without these things, society is a thinner, more ugly, sicker place. You close your libraries, your art galleries, start to make them more difficult to go to, and you close your theatre. I genuinely think that on good nights there we give great parties – I mean, great spiritual parties.

DW: It's not as if there's anything boring or didactic or funless about it, but your plays do give us an experience that enables us to see a better way to live.

AA: I hope so. That's what I would hope comes over. As you say, I don't want to stand there pointing accusing fingers. All one says is that it's not easy, but that we often make fatal mistakes for the best reasons. Most of the time we know the right decision, but sometimes we choose to make the wrong one. All I'm saying is that in the end we live to regret that wrong decision. There is a right way to live.

DW: And it's just something we know instinctively?

AA: Yes we do, I'm sure, most of the time. It's just that we live in an age where everything we used to believe in got turned upside down.

At one stage there was this terrible old patriarchal society where Mr Macmillan was obviously the most honest man in the world; he'd shot a few grouse and things but knew what was good for you. He was like some sort of old uncle, really. And then somebody discovered that there was as much corruption in politics as in the rest of the world. One wasn't so surprised by that, because politicians are representatives of us – we voted them in. But then *everything* became corrupt! I mean everything. We didn't believe in anything. And there was this terrible attitude for a very long time that nothing was worth anything – a completely nihilistic thing.

Now, take a play like *Man of the Moment*, which depicts a direct confrontation between good and evil. It posed a tremendous challenge for me as a dramatist because I knew I could write Vic Parks and make him very entertaining because there's something fascinatingly awful about this snake-like man. I knew that in a sense violence is like a drug – that if I made him physically very violent he could, dangerously, become even more attractive to the audience. Which was when I thought up his relationship with Sharon – a kind of hidden violence, when he attacks her for being fat. A lot of people found that quite unbearable, but I was interested by how much more shocking it was than if he'd taken a piece of wood to her. I don't like to see people beaten up and there's a sort of fascination with it which shouldn't be there. I also wanted to write a good man in Douglas, and found it very hard because good is often seen as rather dull and worthy. In performance, however, I felt the audience stampeding towards Douglas for safety, like Trudy. The thing about Trudy's marriage to Vic is that she went into it with her eye on the main chance. He was a very attractive man with a known violent record, and she chose to take up with him. So that when he is violent to her, she's only got herself to blame. She went in there because at the time it was very glamorous. She went into the relationship for the wrong reasons. Whereas Douglas, who would never attract that sort of adulation, is the bloke who, in the end, she prefers. But I hope I was realistic enough in the end to say that, as long as the human race exists, the Vics of this world will always survive the Douglases.

DW: Quite. So would you say that I'm right in believing that you're not an idealist? The idealising world, when it occurs in your work (*Woman in Mind, Invisible Friends*), very frequently turns bad in some way.

AA: Well those two plays are obviously very closely related, because I rewrote *Woman in Mind* with children in mind. The moral lessons there are almost a memo to myself: instead of trying to make an adjustment in the people you live with, or have to live with, you bypass them and create counterparts. But in the end the problem lies in you. Both those sets of characters are figments of the central woman's imagination, and in all cases they're made in her own image. They're uncontrollable in the end. It's as if she'd cloned herself – and you don't expect clones to be better than the original. Susan has the bigger problem in that she lives with a vicar of the Church of England, Gerald. There's an impregnable calm about Gerald, partly because he has God on his side. All of which generates a residual guilt in her own mind, that every time she kicks a vicar she's getting closer to hell. What makes it even worse is that Gerald is quite adept at turning the other cheek – she could deal with a man who slapped her but a man who just allows himself to be slapped and looks more and more sorrowfully at her is impossible.

DW: He's horrible. He's a sanctimonious character.

AA: But you see, *Woman in Mind* is an interesting play in that it's a first-person narrative. And we get it all from her viewpoint. The first half of the play is all as told by Susan. What I wanted to do was to get the audience to identify with her – to say to them, this is the central character, this is the one I like. There are very few others who you could possibly hope to link with – the dream people are impossible, and there's an awful vicar, and a dreadful sister-in-law. So this woman is all you've really got, besides the barmy doctor who's obviously totally incompetent.

But having stuck with her and getting onto the boat you then realise that you're on a sinking ship, because by the second act you realise, to your horror, that what she's telling us is unreliable. This is confirmed when reality and dream start getting confused: that's a rule you're supposed never to break in playwriting, because it's inconsistent. (It's justified in this case by dramatic effect.) The alarm is first given by Rick, the son, when his real character (as opposed to the character she portrays for us) seems to break through to us.[6] And there are moments towards the end, immediately before she goes into what I call a supernova state, when the whole thing gets very bright and it's like Alice in Wonderland, completely dotty, when you get a glimpse, just for a second, of the real Gerald.[7] There are still a lot of things wrong with him, but we begin to see his point of view – that he is dealing with a woman he doesn't understand because he doesn't recognise mental instability as an illness. This is a very English, middle-class failing; the Americans have trouble understanding it, although they have done the play there. If a guy breaks a leg, fair enough. We can all gather round and get him to hospital and we know what to do. But the number of women who saw that play in London and wrote to Julia McKenzie (who played Susan) saying, 'I went through the same experience and nobody knew'! There was one classic tale of a woman who went with her father. He was in his seventies, she in her forties. He wrote the letter. When the play ended he turned round and she was crying. He was surprised, said he'd had a thoroughly good laugh, and took her to the Savoy to buy her a drink and see what was wrong. She told him that what happened to Susan happened to her. When? She said, 'Ten years ago.' When he said he couldn't remember, she said to him, 'Daddy, you didn't even notice'. She hadn't suffered complete catatonia, but she had gone right down into a state of depression. And he admitted in his letter that he had failed at the time to see it as any sort of problem. That's what Gerald represents.

DW: *Woman in Mind* is tragic; *Henceforward . . .* is tragic; *A Small Family Business* is tragic. What does tragedy consist of, for you?

AA: There is a traditional definition which I suppose I subscribe to, which is that it is to do with choices we make – wrong choices – leading to further wrong choices. I've made a number of choices in my life that I have known to be honourable. (I've also made some very bad choices.) But I've always known when I've made the right choice. And I think tragedy is about not doing that, in its vaguest sense.

I once made a remark that I think is reasonably original – that comedy is a tragedy interrupted: you just stop the drama a fraction before the dénouement. I suppose if the tragedy went on long enough you might get back to comedy again! It is possible to stop most plays at a point where it could go either way.

The way my plays work I just allow them to take their course. The play I'm working on at the moment – it's still very embryonic – is as close to good and evil as I can get. It's about a man who, for the best intentions, chooses the wrong way. I originally wanted to write a play about sponsorship of the arts, but it's wider than that. It's really about how we get into bed with the most extraordinary people. It's set in the middle of a recession, when the spirits are down, and concerns an enthusiastic vicar who decides to revive the mystery plays, to stage them on a huge scale. He's halfway through it when the sponsors drop out. This dark man turns up and offers him some sponsorship – he knows very well who it is! And the man starts altering the script, until you've got Arnold Schwarzenegger slicing people in half, because that's what would appeal to the young.

That's a familiar theme of mine – that the wrong decision is almost right. Very rarely are we confronted with black-and-white choices; usually they're very difficult and demand a lot of thought. But I think in the end there is a way, and if we think about it for a minute we know which way we should go. The danger is that some part of our brain is always there telling us, 'Don't worry, it'll be all right, just this once. Take the £10 note, they're very rich people.' That's the real devil.

Notes and References

1 Introduction: Intangible Commodities

1. These remarkable lines were first published by Jonathan Words-worth, *The Music of Humanity* (London: Nelson, 1969), pp. 269–72, from which they are quoted.
2. Jonathan Wordsworth provides a useful introduction to the millenarian beliefs of the romantics in his Epilogue to *William Wordsworth: The Borders of Vision* (Oxford: Clarendon Press, 1982).
3. Tariq Ali and Howard Brenton, *Moscow Gold* (London: Nick Hern Books, 1990), p. 92.
4. Potter, interviewed by Alan Yentob, *Arena*, BBC2. See also his elucidation of this remark, *Potter on Potter*, ed. Graham Fuller (London: Faber, 1993), p. 86.
5. Howard Brenton, *Diving for Pearls* (London: Nick Hern Books, 1989), p. 223.
6. Alan Bennett, *Forty Years On and Other Plays* (London: Faber, 1991), pp. 10–11.
7. *Forty Years On and Other Plays*, p. 177.
8. *Forty Years On and Other Plays*, p. 154.
9. *Forty Years On and Other Plays*, p. 154.
10. Alan Bennett, *Single Spies* (London: Faber, 1989), p. ix.
11. The success of *Pravda* was a surprise to its authors; see David Hare, 'Sailing Downwind: On *Pravda*', *Writing Left-Handed* (London: Faber, 1991), pp. 132–5.
12. Alan Bennett, *Objects of Affection and Other Plays for Television* (London: British Broadcasting Corporation, 1982), p. 7.
13. Potter, interviewed by Alan Yentob, *Arena*, BBC2.
14. Potter, interviewed by Alan Yentob, *Arena*, BBC2.
15. Simon Gray, *The Holy Terror and Tartuffe* (London: Faber, 1990), p. 40.
16. Simon Gray, *An Unnatural Pursuit and Other Pieces* (London: Faber, 1985), p. 22.
17. *The Holy Terror and Tartuffe*, p. 88.
18. Simon Gray, *Hidden Laughter* (London: Faber, 1990), p. 81.
19. Brenton, interviewed on BBC Radio, 22.8.80.
20. Howard Brenton, *Plays: One* (London: Methuen, 1986), pp. 65–6.
21. Howard Brenton, *The Romans in Britain* (rev. edn, London: Methuen, 1980), p. 86.
22. *The Romans in Britain*, p. 60.
23. *The Romans in Britain*, p. 75.
24. Howard Brenton, *Bloody Poetry* (rev. edn, London: Methuen/Royal Court Writers Series, 1988), pp. 49–50.
25. *The Romans in Britain*, p. 75.
26. David Hare, *Writing Left-Handed* (London: Faber, 1991), p. 159.
27. Howard Brenton, *Berlin Bertie* (London: Nick Hern Books, 1992), p. ix.
28. Brenton and Tom Stoppard, interviewed by John Russell Taylor, BBC Radio, 23 November 1970.

29. David Hare, *Paris By Night* (London: Faber, 1988), p. 71.
30. *Paris By Night*, p. 75.
31. *Writing Left-Handed*, p. 26.
32. I have noted Hare's Wordsworthian tendencies in 'In the air', *New Statesman and Society* (21 June 1991), p. 45.
33. Ayckbourn, interviewed by Duncan Wu, p. 150.
34. Ayckbourn, interviewed by Duncan Wu, p. 150.
35. *The Second Coming*, 5–8.

2   Alan Bennett: Anarchists of the Spirit

1. Alan Bennett, *The Madness of George III* (London: Faber, 1992), p. xx.
2. *The Madness of George III*, pp. xviii-xix.
3. *The Madness of George III*, p. 87.
4. Alan Bennett, *Single Spies* (London: Faber, 1989), p. 48.
5. *Single Spies*, p. viii.
6. *Single Spies*, p. 60.
7. I am grateful to Mr D. Vaisey, Librarian of the Bodleian Library, Oxford, for this information.
8. *Single Spies*, pp. 58–9.
9. *Single Spies*, p. 37.
10. *Single Spies*, pp. 17–18.
11. Interview with S. Simons, transmitted 18 November 1982, BBC Radio Four.
12. *Single Spies*, p. ix.
13. Alan Bennett, *Prick Up Your Ears: The Screenplay* (London: Faber, 1987), p. ix.
14. Alan Bennett, *Talking Heads* (London: British Broadcasting Corporation, 1988), p. 39.
15. *Objects of Affection*, p. 209.
16. *Objects of Affection*, pp. 210–11.
17. Alan Bennett, *The Writer in Disguise* (London: Faber, 1985), p. 59.
18. *The Writer in Disguise*, pp. 71–2.
19. This shamelessly declarative mood is typical of moral revolutionaries in Bennett's work; Mrs Sugden, Orton and Halliwell's landlady in *Prick Up Your Ears*, is a case in point. 'Do you notice I'm limping?' she remarks innocently to them one afternoon, 'Spilt a hot drink over my dress. My vagina came up like a football' (*Prick Up Your Ears*, pp. 19–20).
20. *Talking Heads*, p. 10.
21. *The Writer In Disguise*, p. 37.
22. *The Writer In Disguise*, p. 41.
23. Alan Bennett, *Office Suite* (London: Faber, 1981), p. 8.
24. *The Writer in Disguise*, p. 43.
25. *Talking Heads*, p. 13.
26. *Objects of Affection*, p. 100.
27. *Talking Heads*, p. 53.
28. *Talking Heads*, p. 49.
29. The phrase is Bennett's; *Talking Heads*, p. 7.

30. Alan Bennett, *Two Kafka Plays* (London: Faber, 1987), p. 104.
31. *Two Kafka Plays*, p. 115.
32. *Two Kafka Plays*, p. 123.
33. *Two Kafka Plays*, p. 116.
34. *Two Kafka Plays*, p. 126.
35. *Two Kafka Plays*, pp. 126–7.
36. *Two Kafka Plays*, p. 125.
37. *Two Kafka Plays*, p. 131.
38. *Two Kafka Plays*, p. 13.
39. Bennett discusses his feelings about Orton in the introduction to *Prick Up Your Ears: The Screenplay*.
40. Joe Orton, *Orton: The Complete Plays* (London: Methuen, 1976), p. 26.
41. *Two Kafka Plays*, p. 54.
42. *Two Kafka Plays*, p. 60.
43. 'Reflections on the irrelevance of a Northern upbringing and of a number of other things to the business of being a writer', broadcast 3 May 1976, BBC Radio.
44. *Two Kafka Plays*, p. 12.
45. *Two Kafka Plays*, p. 11.
46. *Two Kafka Plays*, pp. 67–8.
47. *Two Kafka Plays*, p. 55.
48. *Two Kafka Plays*, p. 60.
49. W. H. Auden, *The English Auden* ed. Edward Mendelson (London: Faber, 1977), p. 150.

3 Dennis Potter: The Angel in Us

1. Dennis Potter, *Follow the Yellow Brick Road*, as published in Robert Muller, *The Television Dramatist* (London: Elek, 1973), pp. 303–82, quotation from pp. 331–3.
2. Antonin Artaud, *The Theatre and its Double*, tr. Victor Corti (London: John Calder, 1977), p. 65.
3. Dennis Potter, *Brimstone and Treacle* (London: Methuen, 1978), p. iii.
4. *Follow the Yellow Brick Road*, p. 322.
5. Unedited transcript of interview, *The South Bank Show* production Number 33128, recorded 7 February 1978.
6. Dennis Potter, *The Singing Detective* (London: Faber, 1986), p. 57.
7. Dennis Potter, *Son of Man* (Harmondsworth: Penguin, 1971), p. 66.
8. *Follow the Yellow Brick Road*, p. 370.
9. *Brimstone and Treacle*, p. 2.
10. *Brimstone and Treacle*, p. 2.
11. *Brimstone and Treacle*, p. 3.
12. *Brimstone and Treacle*, p. 3.
13. *Brimstone and Treacle*, p. 15.
14. *Brimstone and Treacle*, p. viii.
15. *Dennis Potter on Television: Waiting for the Boat* (London: Faber, 1984), pp. 33–4.
16. The BBC television serial was transmitted 7 March–11 April 1978; the MGM film adaptation was made in 1981, and the novel was

published in the same year. On the film's failure see *Potter on Potter* ed. Graham Fuller (London: Faber, 1993), pp. 109–11.

17. Dennis Potter, *Pennies From Heaven* (London: Quartet, 1981), p. 39.
18. *Pennies From Heaven*, pp. 49–50.
19. *Pennies From Heaven*, p. 22.
20. *Potter on Potter*, p. 85.
21. *Pennies From Heaven*, p. 106.
22. *Pennies From Heaven*, p. 59.
23. *Pennies From Heaven*, p. 49.
24. *Pennies From Heaven*, p. 146.
25. *Pennies From Heaven*, p. 75.
26. *Pennies From Heaven*, p. 77.
27. *Pennies From Heaven*, p. 73.
28. *Pennies From Heaven*, pp. 145–6.
29. *Pennies From Heaven*, p. 93.
30. *Potter on Potter*, p. 88.
31. *Pennies From Heaven*, p. 132.
32. *Pennies From Heaven*, p. 139.
33. *Pennies From Heaven*, p. 162. It is remarkable, in view of its quality, that the novel of *Pennies From Heaven* was packaged and marketed to tie in with the film.
34. *Pennies From Heaven*, p. 164.
35. *Pennies From Heaven*, pp. 179–80.
36. *Pennies From Heaven*, p. 185.
37. Potter lived in Hammersmith as a child (*Potter on Potter*, p. 7).
38. *Pennies From Heaven*, p. 196.
39. *Waiting for the Boat*, p. 182.
40. Jack's rage may well be analogous to Potter's own frustration at the vulgarisation of *Pennies From Heaven* at the hands of its Hollywood producers.
41. Dennis Potter, *Sufficient Carbohydrate* (London: Faber, 1983), pp. 61–2.
42. See pp. 4–6, above.
43. Potter does not regard drama as an arena for debate about party politics; see *Potter on Potter*, pp. 24–5.
44. *Sufficient Carbohydrate*, p. 30.
45. *Sufficient Carbohydrate*, p. 76.
46. *Sufficient Carbohydrate*, p. 78.
47. Dennis Potter, *Lipstick on Your Collar* (London: Faber, 1993), pp. 155–6.
48. Tim Lott, 'Diamonds in the Dustbin', *New Musical Express* (15 November 1986), p. 31.
49. *Singing Detective*, p. 33.
50. *The Singing Detective*, p. 58.
51. *Brimstone and Treacle*, p. vi.
52. *Singing Detective*, p. 40.
53. *Singing Detective*, p. 57.
54. *Singing Detective*, p. 113.
55. *Singing Detective*, p. 70.
56. *Singing Detective*, p. 232.

57. Ginny Dougary, 'Potter's Weal', *The Times Saturday Review* (26 September 1992), pp. 4–10; p. 8.
58. *Singing Detective*, p. 213.
59. *Singing Detective*, p. 188.
60. *Singing Detective*, p. 188.
61. *Singing Detective*, p. 97.
62. *Singing Detective*, p. 232.
63. *Singing Detective*, p. 211.
64. *Waiting for the Boat*, p. 99.
65. *Singing Detective*, p. 239.
66. *Singing Detective*, p. 211.
67. *Potter on Potter*, p. 91.
68. Dennis Potter, *Blackeyes* (London: Faber, 1987), p. 2.
69. *Blackeyes*, p. 65.
70. *Blackeyes*, p. 48.
71. He quotes (among many other things) *The Prelude*, p. 10, and, shortly before his death, *In Memoriam*, p. 170.
72. *Blackeyes*, p. 12.
73. *Blackeyes*, pp. 43, 45, 46.
74. *Blackeyes*, p. 40.
75. *Blackeyes*, p. 63.
76. *Blackeyes*, p. 134.
77. *Blackeyes*, pp. 63–4.
78. *Blackeyes*, p. 63.
79. *Blackeyes*, p. 48.
80. *Blackeyes*, p. 48.
81. *Blackeyes*, p. 94.
82. *Blackeyes*, p. 49.
83. *Blackeyes*, p. 179.
84. *Blackeyes*, p. 169.
85. Potter on popular music of the 1930s, *Potter on Potter*, p. 86.
86. *Potter on Potter*, p. 87.
87. Dennis Potter, *Lipstick on Your Collar* (London: Faber, 1993), pp. 19–20.
88. *Lipstick on Your Collar*, p. 167.
89. *Lipstick on Your Collar*, p. 174.
90. *Lipstick on Your Collar*, p. 47.
91. *Lipstick on Your Collar*, p. 42.
92. *Singing Detective*, pp. 28–9.
93. *Lipstick on Your Collar*, p. 125.
94. *Lipstick on Your Collar*, p. 75.
95. *Lipstick on Your Collar*, p. 75.
96. This point is underlined by Bernwood's observation that 'If we don't go in, at the right place, in the right manner, and with all the punch it needs, we're done for as a nation and as a people' (*Lipstick on Your Collar*, p. 127).
97. *Lipstick on Your Collar*, p. 143.
98. *Lipstick on Your Collar*, p. 22.
99. *Lipstick on Your Collar*, p. 32.
100. *Potter on Potter*, p. 86

4 Simon Gray: Numbness of the Heart

1. Simon Gray, *Hidden Laughter* (London: Faber, 1990), p. 43.
2. *Hidden Laughter*, p. 2.
3. T. S. Eliot, *Collected Poems 1909–1962* (London: Faber, 1974), p. 190.
4. Simon Gray, *Plays: One* (London: Methuen, 1986), p. 39.
5. Simon Gray, *Otherwise Engaged and Other Plays* (London: Methuen, 1975), p. 36.
6. *Otherwise Engaged and Other Plays*, p. 40.
7. *Otherwise Engaged and Other Plays*, p. 56.
8. *Plays: One*, p. xi.
9. Simon Gray, *The Rear Column and Other Plays* (London: Methuen, 1978), p. 51.
10. *Plays: One*, pp. 240–41.
11. Eliot, *Collected Poems*, p. 78.
12. *Plays: One*, p. 243.
13. *Plays: One*, p. 244.
14. *Plays: One*, p. 222.
15. *Plays: One*, p. 223.
16. *Plays: One*, p. 232.
17. *Plays: One*, pp. 247–8.
18. *Plays: One*, pp. 238–9.
19. *Plays: One*, p. 248.
20. *Plays: One*, p. 254.
21. *Two-Part Prelude* i 290.
22. V, iii, 17–19.
23. Simon Gray, *The Holy Terror and Tartuffe* (London: Faber, 1990), p. 125.
24. *Plays: One*, p. 353.
25. Cf. the infidelity of Jack Barker's wife in *Sufficient Carbohydrate* and that of Philip Marlow in *The Singing Detective*.
26. *The Holy Terror*, pp. 40–41.
27. *Plays: One*, p. 328.
28. *Plays: One*, p. 334.
29. *Plays: One*, p. 346.
30. *The Holy Terror*, p. 48.
31. *The Holy Terror*, p. 46.
32. *The Holy Terror*, p. 72.
33. *Hidden Laughter*, p. 51.
34. *Hidden Laughter*, p. 49.
35. *Hidden Laughter*, p. 74.
36. *Hidden Laughter*, p. 70.
37. *Hidden Laughter*, pp. 78–9.
38. *Hidden Laughter*, p. 58.
39. David Mamet, *Glengarry Glen Ross* (London: Methuen, 1984), p. 24.

5 Howard Brenton: Romantic Retreats

1. Tony Mitchell, *File on Brenton* (London: Methuen, 1987), p. 86.
2. Antonin Artaud, *The Theatre and its Double*, tr. Victor Corti (London: John Calder, 1977), p. 71.

3. 'Our changing theatre'; Tom Stoppard and Howard Brenton interviewed by John Russell Taylor, BBC Radio, transmitted 23 November 1970.
4. Howard Brenton, *Plays: One* (London: Methuen, 1986), p. 27.
5. Among numerous examples see, for instance, Wordsworth, *Thirteen-Book Prelude*, v, 625–9:

> Even forms and substances are circumfused
> By that transparent veil with light divine,
> And through the turnings intricate of verse
> Present themselves as objects recognised
> *In flashes,* and with a glory scarce their own.

6. *Plays: One*, p. 28.
7. *Plays: One*, p. 29.
8. *Plays: One*, p. 345.
9. *Plays: One*, p. 346.
10. Margaretta D'Arcy, *File on Brenton*, p. 37.
11. '3 Plays for Utopia', programme note, Royal Court Theatre, 1988.
12. *Frankenstein*, ed. M. K. Joseph (Oxford: Oxford University Press, 1980), p. 100.
13. *Plays: One*, p. 384.
14. *Plays: One*, p. 376.
15. *Plays: One*, p. 378.
16. *Plays: One*, p. 390.
17. Howard Brenton, *Bloody Poetry* (2nd edn, London: Methuen/Royal Court Writers series, 1988), p. 14.
18. *Bloody Poetry*, p. 37.
19. *Bloody Poetry*, p. 43.
20. *Bloody Poetry*, p. 67.
21. *Bloody Poetry*, p. 80.
22. *Bloody Poetry*, p. 12.
23. Howard Brenton, *Greenland* (London: Methuen/Royal Court Writers Series, 1988), p. 51.
24. *Greenland*, p. 52.
25. Howard Brenton, *Thirteenth Night & A Short Sharp Shock!* (London: Methuen, 1981), pp. 10, 40.
26. *File on Brenton*, p. 50.
27. Howard Brenton, *The Genius* (London: Methuen/Royal Court Writers Series, 1983), p. 35.
28. Bertolt Brecht, *The Life of Galileo*, tr. Howard Brenton (2nd edn, London: Methuen, 1981), p. 85.
29. *The Genius*, p. 37.
30. Howard Brenton, *H.I.D. (Hess is Dead)* (London: Nick Hern Books, 1989), p. 52.
31. *H.I.D.*, p. 53.
32. *H.I.D.*, pp. 56–7.
33. *H.I.D.*, pp. 59–60.
34. Howard Brenton, *Diving for Pearls* (London: Nick Hern Books), p. 159.

35. I have revised the assessment given in my review at the time of the novel's publication; see 'Out of the gutter', *New Statesman and Society* (16 June 1989), p. 37.
36. *Diving for Pearls*, p. 43.
37. V, iii, 311–12.
38. *Diving for Pearls*, p. 223.
39. *Diving for Pearls*, pp. 24–5.
40. *Diving for Pearls*, pp. 26, 202.
41. *H.I.D.*, pp. 66–7. It is interesting how closely Brenton's reflections on human nature in the post-communist era parallel those of Ian McEwan, *Black Dogs* (London: Jonathan Cape, 1992).
42. Tariq Ali and Howard Brenton, *Iranian Nights* (London: Nick Hern Books, 1989).
43. Tariq Ali and Howard Brenton, *Moscow Gold* (London: Nick Hern Books, 1990), p. 90.
44. *Moscow Gold*, p. 19.
45. *Moscow Gold*, p. 69.
46. *Moscow Gold*, p. 1.
47. *Moscow Gold*, p. 85.
48. *Moscow Gold*, p. 92.
49. *Moscow Gold*, p. 83.
50. *Moscow Gold*, p. 88.
51. Howard Brenton, *Berlin Bertie* (London: Nick Hern Books/Royal Court Programme, 1992), p. 55.
52. *Plays: One*, p. 370.
53. *Berlin Bertie*, p. 31.
54. *Berlin Bertie*, p. 59.
55. *Berlin Bertie*, p. 49.
56. *Berlin Bertie*, p. 66.
57. This is a quotation, of course, from *The Defence of Poetry*.
58. *Berlin Bertie*, p. 67.
59. *Berlin Bertie*, p. 71.
60. *Berlin Bertie*, p. 70.
61. *Berlin Bertie*, p. 53.
62. *Berlin Bertie*, p. 58.
63. *Berlin Bertie*, p. 54.
64. D. H. Lawrence, *Apocalypse* (London: Heinemann, 1972), p. 42.
65. Quoted by Carole Angier, 'Defender of the memory', *The Guardian* (18 November 1992), G2 Arts 4/5, p. 5.

6 David Hare: A Milder Day

1. Howard Brenton and David Hare, *Pravda* (2nd edn, London: Methuen, 1986), pp. 106–7.
2. David Hare, *The History Plays* (London: Faber, 1984), p. 188.
3. *History Plays*, p. 141.
4. *History Plays*, p. 207.
5. *History Plays*, p. 193.

6. *History Plays*, pp. 193–4.
7. Malcolm Page, *File on Hare* (London: Methuen, 1990), p. 43.
8. *File on Hare*, p. 44.
9. *History Plays*, p. 199.
10. *History Plays*, p. 203.
11. *History Plays*, p. 203.
12. *History Plays*, p. 196.
13. *History Plays*, p. 204.
14. David Hare, *Heading Home, Wetherby and Dreams of Leaving* (London: Faber, 1991), p. 123.
15. *Heading Home*, p. 112.
16. *Heading Home*, p. 102.
17. William Wordsworth, *The Ruined Cottage and The Pedlar*, ed. James Butler (Ithaca, NY: Cornell University Press, 1978), p. 157.
18. *File on Hare*, p. 61.
19. *Heading Home*, p. 113.
20. *Heading Home*, pp. 128–9.
21. Wordsworth's *Prelude*, Book VIII, was entitled 'Love of Nature leading to Love of Mankind', the philosophical principle on which he based his epic, *The Recluse*.
22. *Heading Home*, p. 78.
23. David Hare, *Strapless* (London: Faber, 1989), p. 72.
24. *Strapless*, p. 79.
25. V, iii, 17–19.
26. V, iii, 307–8.
27. *Heading Home*, p. 15.
28. This is cogently discussed by Jonathan Wordsworth, *William Wordsworth: The Borders of Vision* (Oxford: Clarendon Press, 1982), Chapter Seven. Hyperlinguistic communication is characteristic of many such parareligious sects; Madame Blavatsky, guru to Yeats and Kandinsky among others, envisaged a similar 'immaterial' language based on 'thought forms'.
29. *Heading Home*, p. 25.
30. *Heading Home*, p. 36.
31. *Heading Home*, p. 35.
32. *Heading Home*, p. 37.
33. *Heading Home*, p. 55.
34. *Heading Home*, p. 65.
35. *Heading Home*, p. 66.
36. David Hare, *The Secret Rapture* (London: Faber, 1988), p. 38.
37. *Secret Rapture*, p. 68.
38. David Hare, *Paris by Night* (London: Faber, 1988), p. 58.
39. *Paris by Night*, p. 82.
40. *Paris by Night*, p. 82.
41. For *The Spectator*, c.1970; see *File on Hare*, p. 84. *Knuckle* (1974) was apparently inspired by Macdonald's work; see *History Plays*, p. 11.
42. *Secret Rapture*, p. 17.
43. *Secret Rapture*, p. 5.
44. *Secret Rapture*, p. 40.

45. *Secret Rapture*, p. 70.
46. *Secret Rapture*, pp. 82–3.
47. *File on Hare*, pp. 74–5.
48. V, iii, 313.
49. V, iii, 314–15.
50. Quoted from A. Norman Jeffares, *A New Commentary on the Poems of W. B. Yeats* (London: Macmillan, 1984), p. 364.
51. *Lapis Lazuli*, 12–17.
52. *Secret Rapture*, p. 83.
53. David Hare, *Asking Around: Background to the David Hare Trilogy* (London: Faber, 1993), p. 8.
54. David Hare, *Racing Demon* (London: Faber, 1990), p. 3.
55. *Racing Demon*, p. 52.
56. In *Knuckle* (1974) it is 'one of Surrey's contagious diseases', according to a Guildfordian (*History Plays*, p. 30).
57. David Hare, *Murmuring Judges* (London: Faber, 1991), p. 83.
58. *Murmuring Judges*, p. 82.
59. *Secret Rapture*, p. 48.
60. *Murmuring Judges*, p. 85.
61. IV, vi, 164–5.
62. *Racing Demon*, p. 79.
63. *Racing Demon*, p. 54.
64. *Racing Demon*, p. 56.
65. *File on Hare*, p. 83.
66. *Racing Demon*, p. 88.
67. David Hare, *The Absence of War* (London: Faber, 1993), pp. 18–19.
68. *Absence of War*, p. 104.
69. *Absence of War*, p. 20.
70. *Absence of War*, p. 18.
71. *Absence of War*, p. 91.
72. *Absence of War*, p. 4.
73. *Absence of War*, p. 53.
74. *Asking Around*, p. 221.
75. *Absence of War*, p. 92.
76. *Absence of War*, p. 97.
77. *Absence of War*, p. 50.
78. *Heading Home*, p. 123.
79. *Asking Around*, p. 237.
80. *Absence of War*, p. 15.
81. *Asking Around*, p. 206.
82. *Absence of War*, p. 49.
83. *Absence of War*, pp. 47–8.
84. *Absence of War*, p. 49.

7 Alan Ayckbourn: Beyond Romanticism

1. Alan Ayckbourn, *Man of the Moment* (London: Faber, 1990), p. 31.
2. The phrase is Simon Trussler's, who also goes on to qualify it; see Malcolm Page, *File on Ayckbourn* (London: Methuen, 1989), p. 6.

3. Alan Ayckbourn interviewed by Duncan Wu, p. 151.
4. *Man of the Moment*, pp. 12–13.
5. *Man of the Moment*, pp. 69–70.
6. Ayckbourn, interviewed by Duncan Wu, p. 151.
7. *Man of the Moment*, p. 63.
8. *Man of the Moment*, p. 52.
9. *Man of the Moment*, p. 19.
10. *Man of the Moment*, p. 71.
11. Alan Ayckbourn, *A Chorus of Disapproval* (London: Faber, 1986), p. 21.
12. *Chorus of Disapproval*, p. 22.
13. *Chorus of Disapproval*, pp. 74–5.
14. *Chorus of Disapproval*, p. 22.
15. *Chorus of Disapproval*, pp. 33–4.
16. *King Lear*, IV, vi, 158–9, 165.
17. *Chorus of Disapproval*, p. 77.
18. *Chorus of Disapproval*, p. 25.
19. *Chorus of Disapproval*, pp. 76–7.
20. Seamus Heaney, *The Cure at Troy: A Version of Sophocles' Philoctetes* (London: Faber, 1990), p. 77.
21. *Chorus of Disapproval*, p. 23.
22. *Chorus of Disapproval*, p. 32.
23. *Chorus of Disapproval*, p. 76.
24. Ayckbourn, interviewed by Duncan Wu, p. 146.
25. *Chorus of Disapproval*, p. 94.
26. *Chorus of Disapproval*, p. 95.
27. Alan Ayckbourn, *Woman in Mind* (London: Faber, 1986), p. 16.
28. *Woman in Mind*, p. 82.
29. *Woman in Mind*, p. 39.
30. *File on Ayckbourn*, p. 75.
31. *File on Ayckbourn*, p. 89.
32. *Woman in Mind*, p. 35.
33. *Woman in Mind*, p. 59.
34. *Woman in Mind*, p. 81.
35. See p. 5, above.
36. Ayckbourn, interviewed by Duncan Wu, p. 154.
37. Alan Ayckbourn, *Henceforward . . .* (London: Faber, 1988), p. 38.
38. *Henceforward . . .*, p. 37.
39. *Henceforward . . .*, p. 86.
40. *Henceforward . . .*, p. 89.
41. *Henceforward . . .*, p. 94.
42. *Henceforward . . .*, p. 39.
43. Ayckbourn, interviewed by Duncan Wu, p. 149.
44. *Henceforward . . .*, p. 96.
45. Ayckbourn, interviewed by Duncan Wu, p. 149.
46. Alan Ayckbourn, *A Small Family Business* (London: Faber, 1987), p. 34
47. *A Small Family Business*, p. 8.
48. *A Small Family Business*, p. 11.
49. *A Small Family Business*, p. 9.
50. *A Small Family Business*, pp. 111–12.

51. Alan Ayckbourn, *The Revengers' Comedies* (London: Faber, 1991), p. 12.
52. *Revengers' Comedies*, pp. 12–13.
53. Tariq Ali and Howard Brenton, *Moscow Gold* (London: Nick Hern Books, 1990), p. 92.
54. *Revengers' Comedies*, p. 20.
55. *Revengers' Comedies*, pp. 177–8.
56. Jean-Jacques Rousseau, *The Social Contract* tr. Maurice Cranston (Harmondsworth: Penguin, 1968), p. 49.
57. Alan Ayckbourn, *Time of My Life* (London: Faber, 1993), pp. 100–101.
58. *Time of My Life*, p. 92.
59. *Time of My Life*, p. 67.
60. *Time of My Life*, pp. 46–7.
61. *Time of My Life*, p. 91.
62. *Time of My Life*, p. 12.
63. 'You know how I feel about babies', she tells him, 'I managed with my own - just . . .' (*Time of My Life*, p. 77).
64. *Time of My Life*, p. 93.
65. *Time of My Life*, p. 27.
66. *Time of My Life*, p. 50.
67. *Time of My Life*, pp. 36–7.
68. *Time of My Life*, p. 67.
69. *Time of My Life*, p. 75.
70. *Time of My Life*, p. 75.
71. *Time of My Life*, p. 17.
72. *Time of My Life*, p. 92.
73. *Time of My Life*, p. 65.
74. *Time of My Life*, p. 66.
75. *Time of My Life*, p. 31.
76. *Time of My Life*, p. 51.
77. *Time of My Life*, pp. 99–100.
78. *File on Ayckbourn*, p. 78.
79. Just how true this is, is revealed in a letter Larkin wrote on the day he killed the hedgehog, in which he notes that 'This has been rather a depressing day: killed a hedgehog when mowing the lawn, by accident of course. It's upset me rather' (*Selected Letters of Philip Larkin 1940–1985*, ed. Anthony Thwaite [London: Faber, 1992], p. 601).
80. Philip Larkin, *Collected Poems*, ed. Anthony Thwaite (London: Faber, 1988), p. 214.

8   Epilogue

1. *The Second Wave: British Drama for the Seventies* (London: Methuen, 1971), p. 225.
2. Richard Brooks, 'Fearless Potter fumes to the last', *Observer*, 27 March 1994, p. 8. Further comments by Potter on the hopelessness of British television may be found in *Potter on Potter*, p. 140. He puts the blame on Rupert Murdoch – Rupert being the name he is reported to have given his cancer-ridden pancreas.
3. *The Second Wave*, p. 227.

4. At the time of writing (March 1994), the official London theatre guide lists only three original plays in the West End to have opened in the last year. Alongside them, there are revivals of *An Inspector Calls*, *Travesties*, *Piaf*, *A Month in the Country* and *September Tide*.
5. *File on Hare*, p. 81.
6. *The Ideology of the Aesthetic* (Oxford: Blackwell, 1990), p. 412.

Appendix   An Interview with Alan Ayckbourn

1. Watson does touch on the subject, albeit briefly, p. 90.
2. *Chorus of Disapproval*, p. 95.
3. *A Small Family Business*, pp. 7–8.
4. *A Small Family Business*, pp. 111–12.
5. *Henceforward . . .*, pp. 97–8.
6. *Woman in Mind*, pp. 51–6.
7. *Woman in Mind*, pp. 76–8

Bibliography

Ali, Tariq and Howard Brenton, *Moscow Gold* (London: Nick Hern Books, 1990)

——, *Iranian Nights* (London: Nick Hern Books, 1989)

Angier, Carole, 'Defender of the memory', *The Guardian* (18 November 1992), GS Arts 4/5, p. 5

Artaud, Antonin, *The Theatre and its Double*, tr. Victor Corti (London: John Calder, 1977)

Auden, W. H., *The English Auden: Poems, Essays, and Dramatic Writings, 1927–1939*, ed. Edward Mendelson (London: Faber, 1977)

Ayckbourn, Alan, *The Norman Conquests* (Harmondsworth: Penguin, 1977)

——, *A Chorus of Disapproval* (London: Faber, 1986)

——, *Woman in Mind* (London: Faber, 1986)

——, *A Small Family Business* (London: Faber, 1987)

——, *Henceforward . . .* (London: Faber, 1988)

——, *Man of the Moment* (London: Faber, 1990)

——, *The Revengers' Comedies* (London: Faber, 1991)

——, *Time of My Life* (London: Faber, 1993)

——, *Wildest Dreams* (London: Faber, 1993)

Bennett, Alan, *Office Suite* (London: Faber, 1981)

——, *Objects of Affection and other plays for television* (London: BBC, 1982)

——, *A Private Function* (London: Faber, 1984)

——, *The Writer in Disguise* (London: Faber, 1985)

——, *Prick Up Your Ears: The Screenplay* (London: Faber, 1987)

——, *Two Kafka Plays* (London: Faber, 1987)

——, *Talking Heads* (London: BBC, 1988)

——, *Single Spies* (London: Faber, 1989)

——, *The Lady in the Van* (London: London Review of Books, 1990)

——, *Forty Years on and Other Plays* (London: Faber, 1991)

——, *The Madness of George III* (London: Faber, 1992)

Brecht, Bertolt, *The Life of Galileo* tr. Howard Brenton (2nd edn, London: Methuen, 1981)

Brenton, Howard, *Thirteenth Night & A Short Sharp Shock!* (London: Methuen, 1981)

——, *The Genius* (London: Methuen/Royal Court Writers series, 1983)

——, *Plays: One* (London: Methuen, 1986)

——, *Bloody Poetry* (2nd edn, London: Methuen/Royal Court Writers series, 1988)

——, *Greenland* (London: Methuen/Royal Court Writers series, 1988)

——, '3 Plays for Utopia', programme note, Royal Court Theatre, 1988

——, *Diving for Pearls* (London: Nick Hern Books, 1989)

——, *H.I.D. (Hess is Dead)* (London: Nick Hern Books, 1989)

——, *Berlin Bertie* (London: Nick Hern Books, 1992)

Brenton, Howard and David Hare, *Pravda* (2nd edn, London: Methuen, 1986)

Brooks, Richard, 'A silly habit for a grown-up', *The Observer* (6 December 1992), p. 61

——, 'Fearless Potter fumes to the last', *The Observer* (27 March 1994), p. 8

Churchill, Caryl, *Serious Money* (London: Methuen/Royal Court Writers series, 1987)

Dougary, Ginny, 'Potter's Weal', *The Times Saturday Review* (26 September 1992), pp. 4–10

Eagleton, Terry, *The Ideology of the Aesthetic* (Oxford: Blackwell, 1990)

Eliot, T. S., *Collected Poems 1909–1962* (London: Faber, 1974)

Fuller, Graham (ed.), *Potter on Potter* (London: Faber, 1993)

Gray, Simon, *Otherwise Engaged and Other Plays* (London: Methuen, 1975)

——, *The Common Pursuit* (London: Methuen, 1984).

——, *An Unnatural Pursuit and other pieces* (London: Faber, 1985)

——, *Little Portia* (London: Faber, 1986)

——, *Plays: One* (London: Methuen, 1986)

——, *Melon* (London: Methuen, 1987)

——, *Hidden Laughter* (London: Faber, 1990)

——, *The Holy Terror and Tartuffe* (London: Faber, 1990)

——, *The Definitive Simon Gray* (3 vols, London: Faber, 1991–3)

Hare, David, *The Asian Plays* (London: Faber, 1984)

——, *The History Plays* (London: Faber, 1984)

——, *Paris by Night* (London: Faber, 1988)

——, *The Secret Rapture* (London: Faber, 1988)

——, *Strapless* (London: Faber, 1989)

——, *Racing Demon* (London: Faber, 1990)

——, *Heading Home, Wetherby and Dreams of Leaving* (London: Faber, 1991)

——, *Murmuring Judges* (London: Faber, 1991)

——, *Writing Left-Handed* (London: Faber, 1991)

——, *The Absence of War* (London: Faber, 1993)

——, *Asking Around: Background to the David Hare Trilogy* (London: Faber, 1993)

Heaney, Seamus, *The Cure at Troy: A Version of Sophocles' Philoctetes* (London: Faber, 1990)

Jeffares, A. Norman, *A New Commentary on the Poems of W. B. Yeats* (London: Macmillan, 1984)

Larkin, Philip, *Collected Poems* (London: Faber, 1988)

——, *Selected Letters of Philip Larkin 1940–1985*, ed. Anthony Thwaite (London: Faber, 1992)

Lawrence, D. H., *Apocalypse* (London: Heinemann, 1972)

Lott, Tim, 'Diamonds in the Dustbin', *New Musical Express* (15 November 1986), p. 31

McEwan, Ian, *Black Dogs* (London: Jonathan Cape, 1992)

Mamet, David, *Glengarry Glen Ross* (London: Methuen, 1984)

Mitchell, Tony, *File on Brenton* (London: Methuen, 1987)

Orton, Joe, *Orton: The Complete Plays* (London: Methuen, 1976)

Page, Malcolm, *File on Ayckbourn* (London: Methuen, 1989)

——, *File on Hare* (London: Methuen, 1990)

Potter, Dennis, *The Nigel Barton Plays: Stand Up, Nigel Barton; Vote Vote Vote for Nigel Barton* (Harmondsworth: Penguin, 1967)

——, *Son of Man* (Harmondsworth: Penguin, 1971)

——, *Follow the Yellow Brick Road*, in Robert Muller (ed.), *The Television Dramatist* (London: Elek, 1973), pp. 303–82

——, *Brimstone and Treacle* (London: Methuen, 1978)

——, *Pennies From Heaven* (London: Quartet, 1981)

——, *Sufficient Carbohydrate* (London: Faber, 1983)

——, *Dennis Potter on Television: Waiting for the Boat* (London: Faber, 1984)

——, *The Singing Detective* (London: Faber, 1986)

——, *Blackeyes* (London: Faber, 1987)

——, *Lipstick on Your Collar* (London: Faber, 1993)

Priestley, J. B., *An Inspector Calls* (London: Samuel French, 1948)

Shakespeare, William, *The Riverside Shakespeare*, ed. G. Blakemore Evans (Boston, Mass.: Houghton Mifflin, 1974)

Shelley, Mary, *Frankenstein*, ed. M. K. Joseph (London: Oxford University Press, 1980)

Taylor, John Russell, *The Second Wave: British Drama for the Seventies* (London: Methuen, 1971)

Tennyson, Alfred Lord, *The Poems of Tennyson*, ed. Christopher Ricks (London: Longman, 1969)

Watson, Ian, *Conversations with Ayckbourn* (rev. edn, London: Faber, 1988)

Wordsworth, Jonathan, *The Music of Humanity* (London: Nelson, 1969)

——, *William Wordsworth: The Borders of Vision* (Oxford: Clarendon Press, 1982)

Wordsworth, William, *The Ruined Cottage and The Pedlar*, ed. James Butler (Ithaca, NY: Cornell University Press, 1978)

——, *The Prelude: 1799, 1805, 1850* ed. Jonathan Wordsworth, Stephen Gill and M. H. Abrams (New York: W. W. Norton, 1979)

——, *Poems in Two Volumes, and Other Poems, 1800–1807*, ed. Jared Curtis (Ithaca, NY: Cornell University Press, 1983)

——, *The Oxford Poetry Library Wordsworth* ed. Stephen Gill and Duncan Wu (Oxford: Oxford University Press, 1994)

Wu, Duncan, 'Realistic Revolutions' (review of Howard Brenton, *Bloody Poetry*, Royal Court Theatre), *TLS*, 22–8 April 1988

——, 'In search of Utopia' (review of Howard Brenton, *Sore Throats* and *Greenland*, Royal Court Theatre), *TLS*, 17–23 June 1988

——, 'Out of the gutter' (review of *Diving for Pearls*), *New Statesman and Society* (16 June 1989), p. 37

——, 'In the air' (review of *Writing Left-Handed*), *New Statesman and Society* (21 June 1991)

Yeats, W. B., *The Collected Poems of W. B. Yeats* (London: Macmillan, 1950)

——, *The Poems: A New Edition*, ed. Richard J. Finneran (London: Macmillan, 1984)

Index